OFF TO THE RACES! SECRETARIAT AND THE TRIPLE CROWN

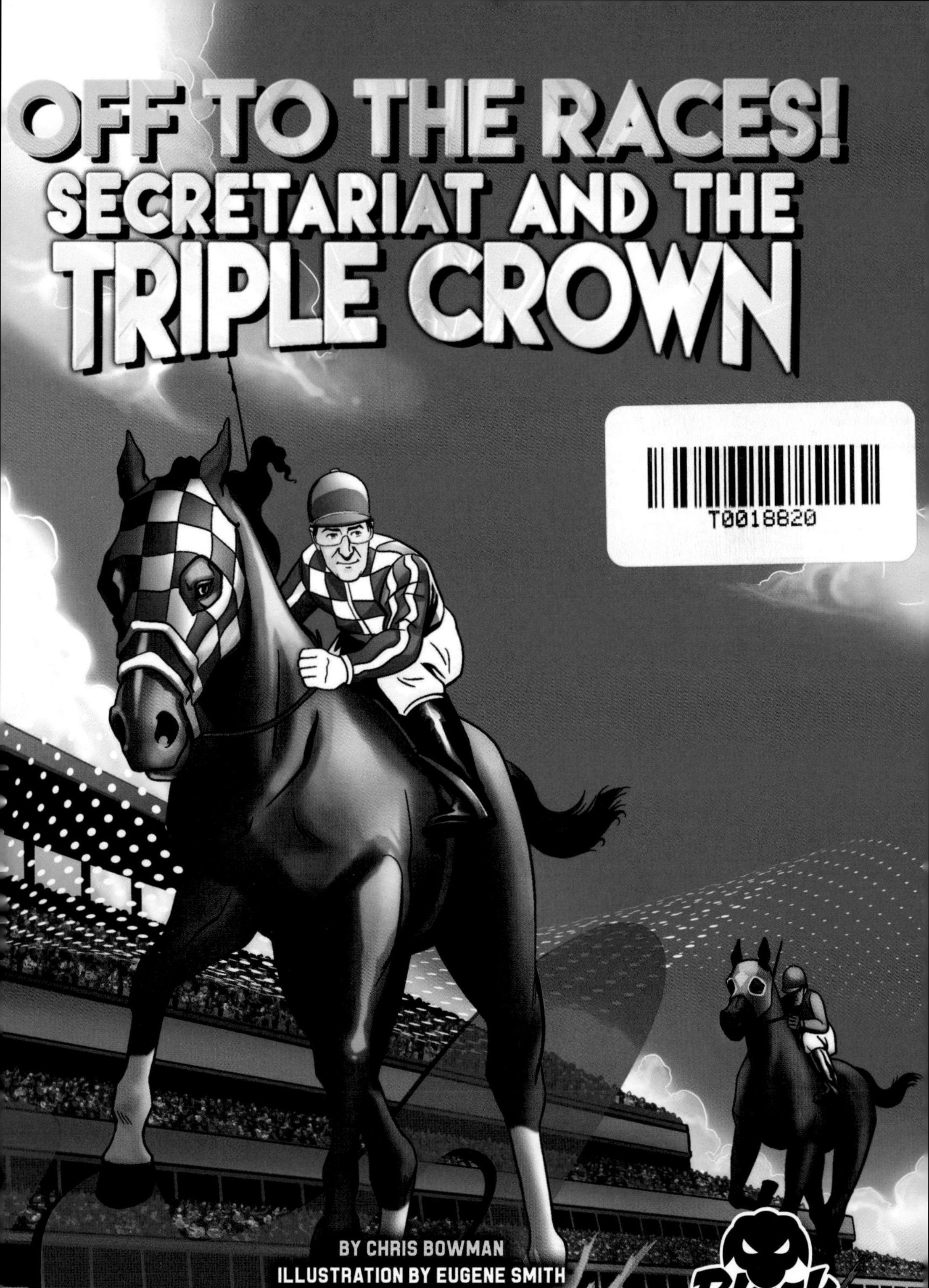

BY CHRIS BOWMAN
ILLUSTRATION BY EUGENE SMITH
COLOR BY GERARDO SANDOVAL

Black Sheep

BELLWETHER MEDIA • MINNEAPOLIS, MN

STRAY FROM REGULAR READS WITH BLACK SHEEP BOOKS. FEEL A RUSH WITH EVERY READ!

This edition first published in 2024 by Bellwether Media, Inc.

No part of this publication may be reproduced in whole or in part without written permission of the publisher. For information regarding permission, write to Bellwether Media, Inc., Attention: Permissions Department, 6012 Blue Circle Drive, Minnetonka, MN 55343.

Library of Congress Cataloging-in-Publication Data

Names: Bowman, Chris, 1990- author.
Title: Off to the races! : Secretariat and the Triple Crown / by Chris Bowman.
Other titles: Secretariat and the Triple Crown
Description: Minneapolis, MN : Bellwether Media, [2024] | Series: Greatest moments in sports | Includes bibliographical references and index. | Audience: Ages 7-13 | Audience: Grades 4-6 | Summary: "Exciting illustrations follow the events of Secretariat racing the Triple Crown. The combination of brightly colored panels and leveled text is intended for students in grades 3 through 8" Provided by publisher.
Identifiers: LCCN 2023017802 (print) | LCCN 2023017803 (ebook) | ISBN 9798886875096 (library binding) | ISBN 9798886875591 (paperback) | ISBN 9798886876970 (ebook)
Subjects: LCSH: Secretariat (Horse), 1970-1989–Juvenile literature. | Triple Crown (U.S. horse racing)–Juvenile literature. | Race horses–United States–Biography–Juvenile literature.
Classification: LCC SF355.S42 B69 2023 (print) | LCC SF355.S42 (ebook) | DDC 798.40092/9 [B]–dc23/eng/20230515
LC record available at https://lccn.loc.gov/2023017802
LC ebook record available at https://lccn.loc.gov/2023017803

Editor: Betsy Rathburn   Designer: Andrea Schneider

Printed in the United States of America, North Mankato, MN.

TABLE OF CONTENTS

Red text identifies historical quotes.

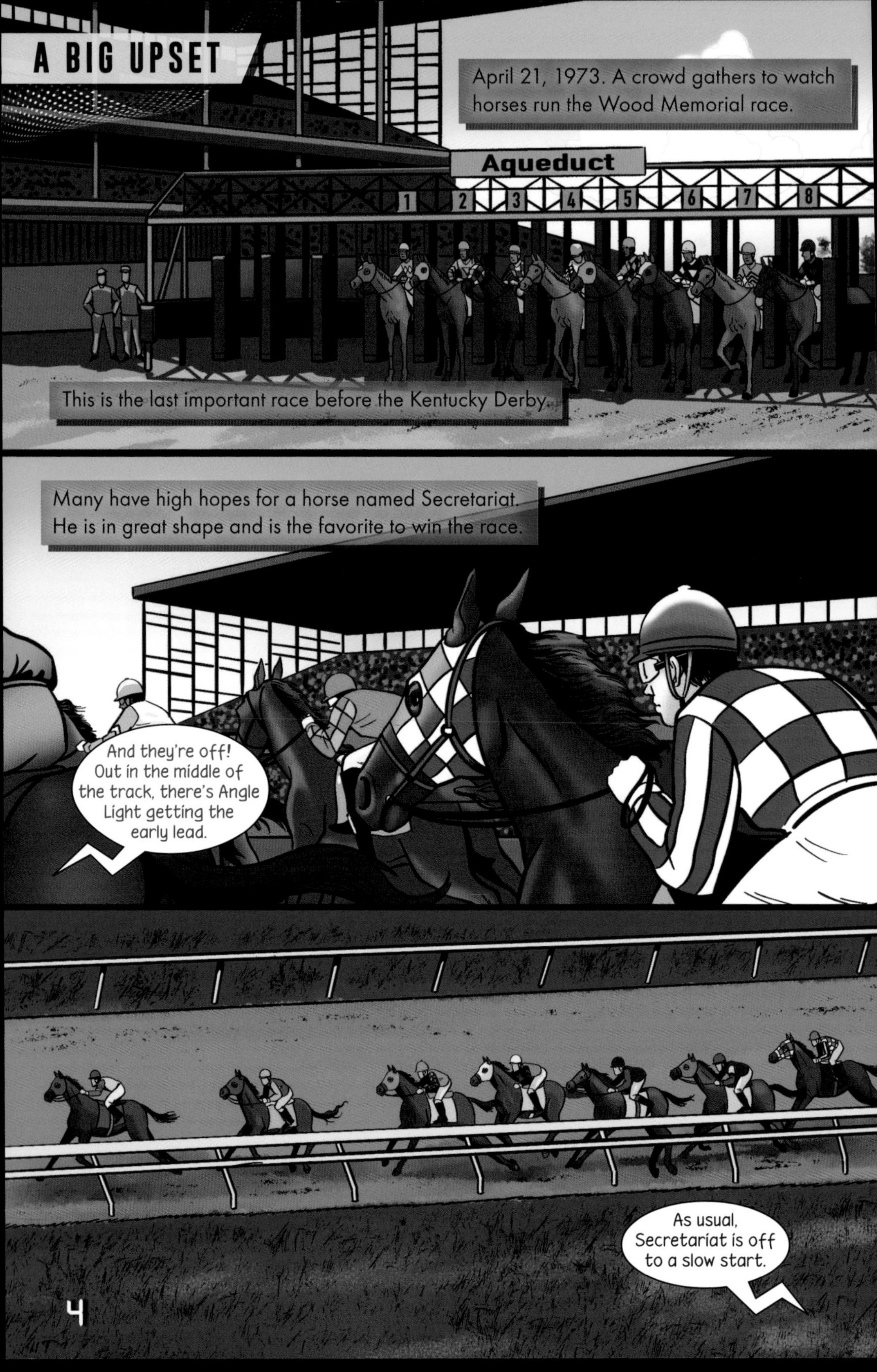
A BIG UPSET
April 21, 1973. A crowd gathers to watch horses run the Wood Memorial race.
Aqueduct
1 2 3 4 5 6 7 8
This is the last important race before the Kentucky Derby.
Many have high hopes for a horse named Secretariat. He is in great shape and is the favorite to win the race.
And they're off! Out in the middle of the track, there's Angle Light getting the early lead.
As usual, Secretariat is off to a slow start.

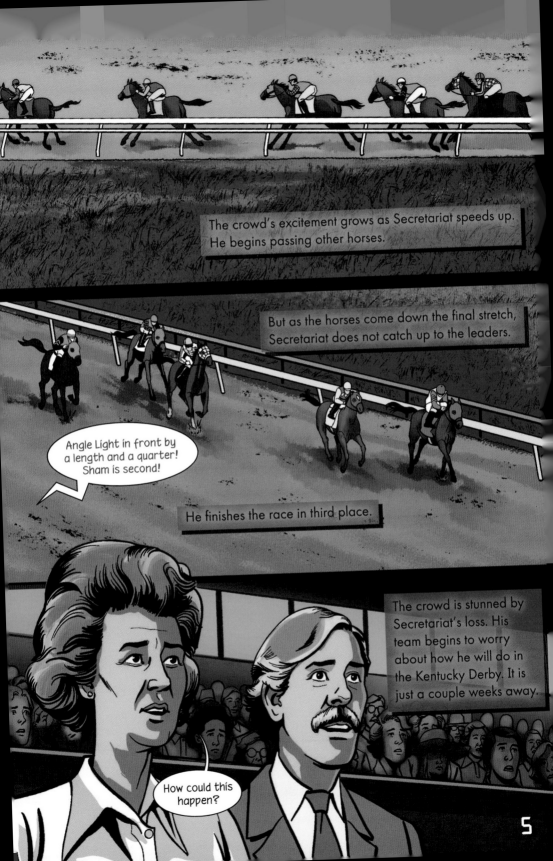

The crowd's excitement grows as Secretariat speeds up. He begins passing other horses.

But as the horses come down the final stretch, Secretariat does not catch up to the leaders.

Angle Light in front by a length and a quarter! Sham is second!

He finishes the race in third place.

The crowd is stunned by Secretariat's loss. His team begins to worry about how he will do in the Kentucky Derby. It is just a couple weeks away.

How could this happen?

THE FLIP OF A COIN

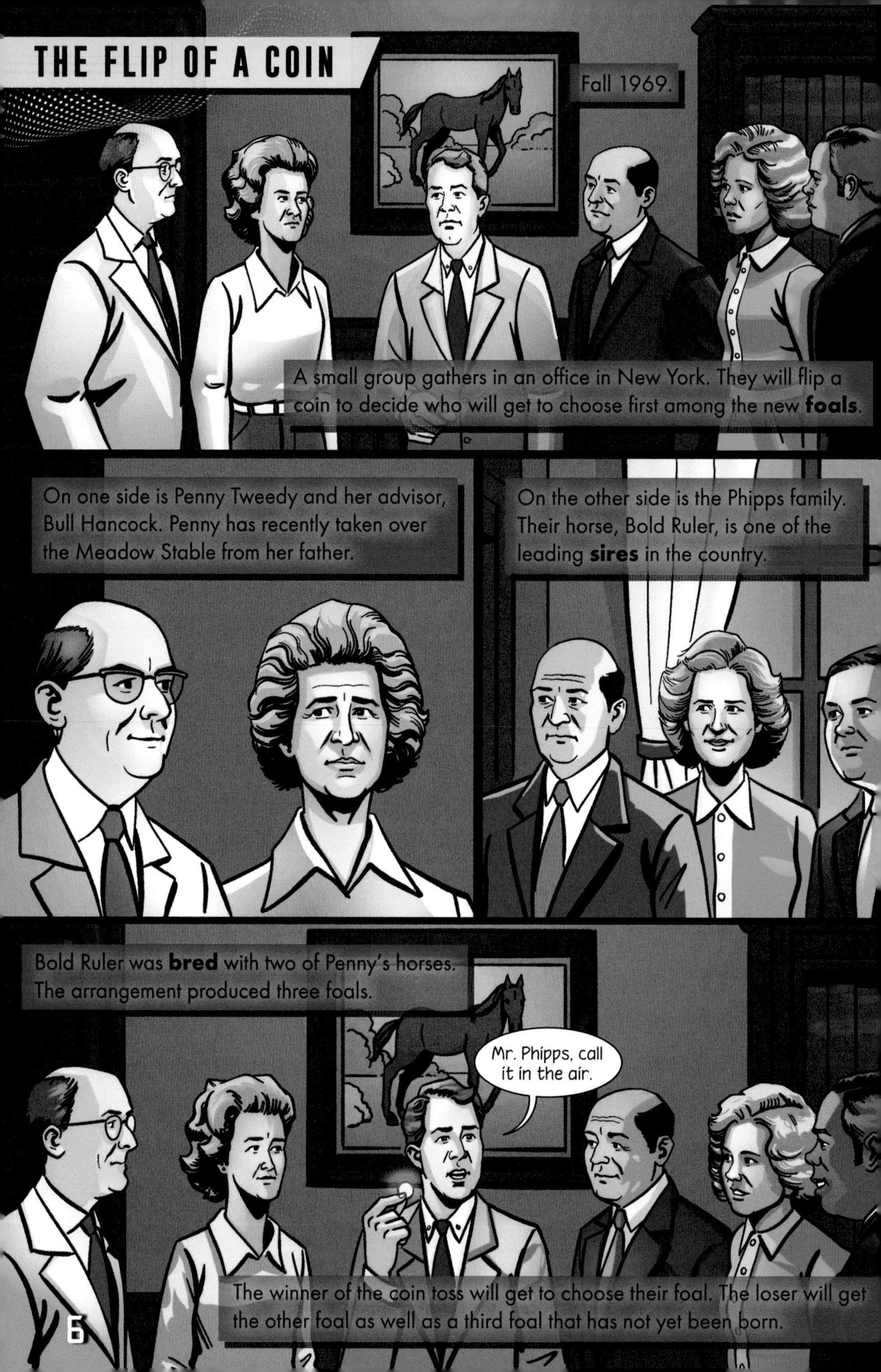
Fall 1969.
A small group gathers in an office in New York. They will flip a coin to decide who will get to choose first among the new **foals**.
On one side is Penny Tweedy and her advisor, Bull Hancock. Penny has recently taken over the Meadow Stable from her father.
On the other side is the Phipps family. Their horse, Bold Ruler, is one of the leading **sires** in the country.
Bold Ruler was **bred** with two of Penny's horses. The arrangement produced three foals.
Mr. Phipps, call it in the air.
The winner of the coin toss will get to choose their foal. The loser will get the other foal as well as a third foal that has not yet been born.

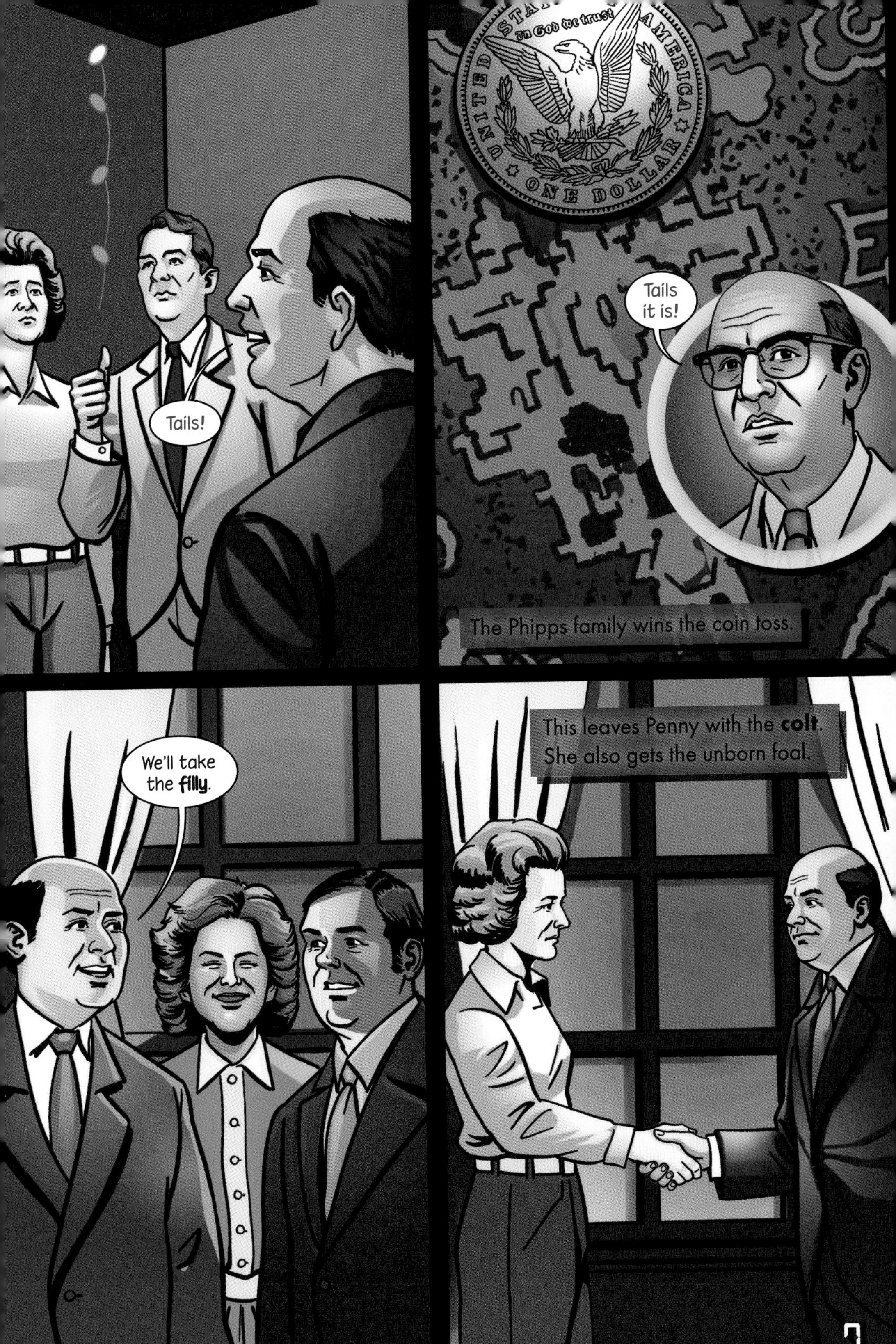

Tails!
In God we trust
UNITED STATES OF AMERICA
ONE DOLLAR
Tails it is!
The Phipps family wins the coin toss.
We'll take the **filly**.
This leaves Penny with the **colt**. She also gets the unborn foal.

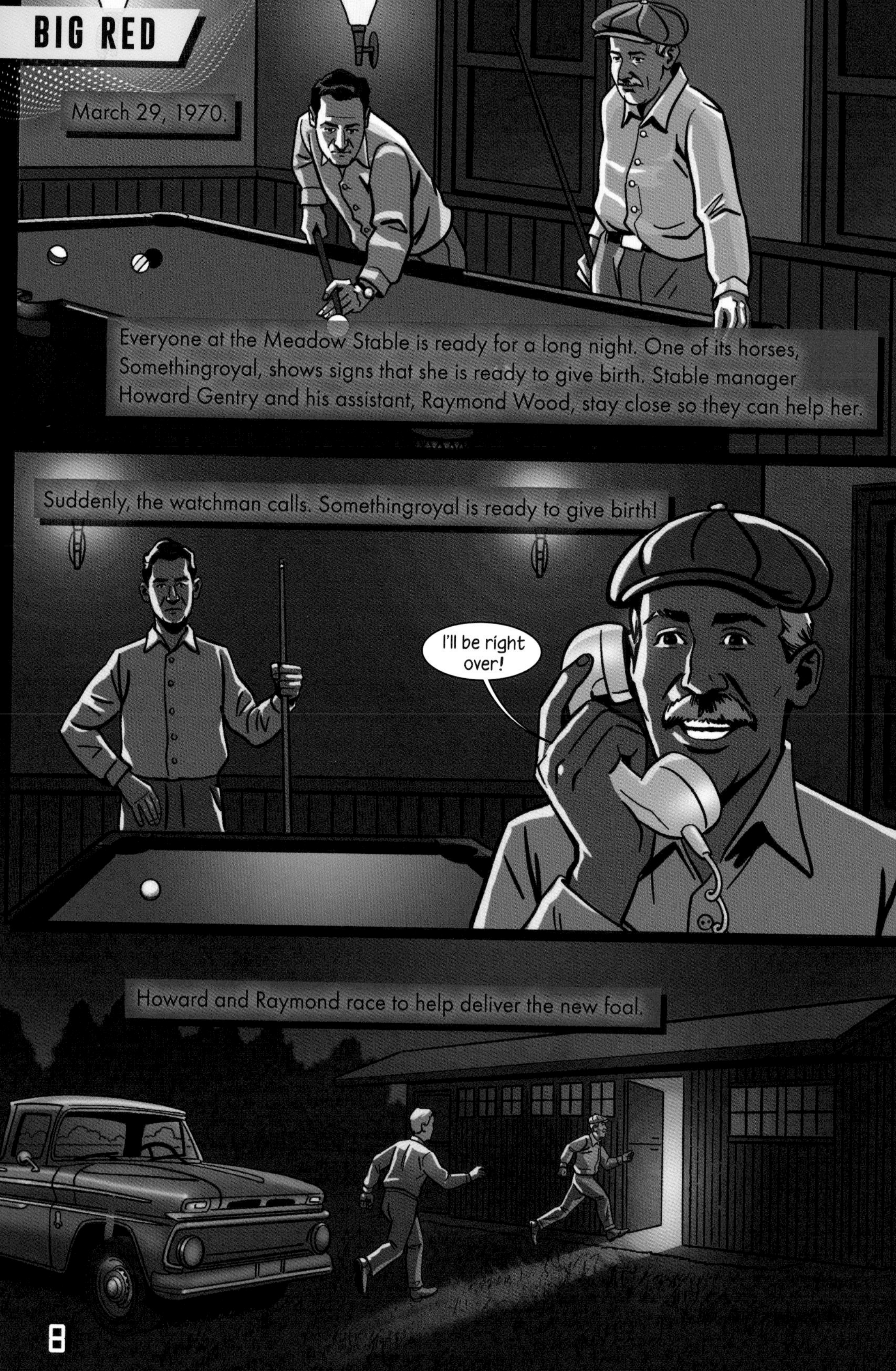
March 29, 1970.
Everyone at the Meadow Stable is ready for a long night. One of its horses, Somethingroyal, shows signs that she is ready to give birth. Stable manager Howard Gentry and his assistant, Raymond Wood, stay close so they can help her.
Suddenly, the watchman calls. Somethingroyal is ready to give birth!
I'll be right over!
Howard and Raymond race to help deliver the new foal.

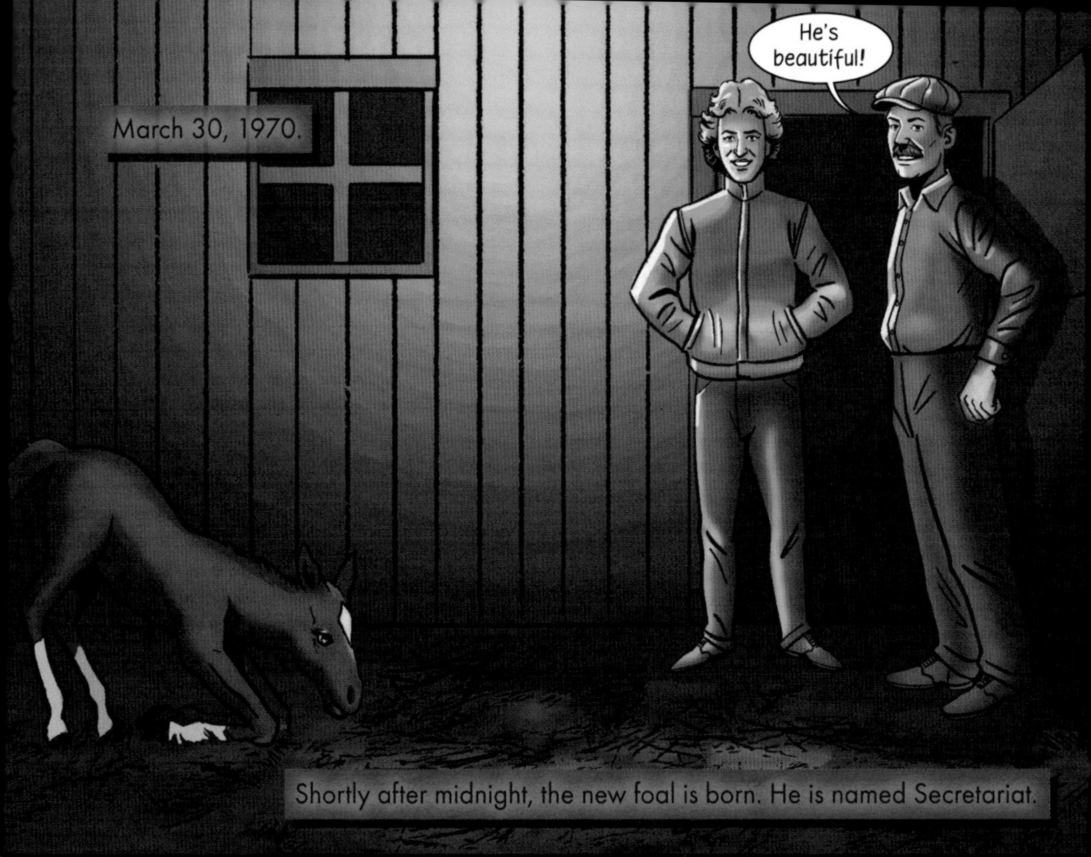
March 30, 1970.
He's beautiful!
Shortly after midnight, the new foal is born. He is named Secretariat.

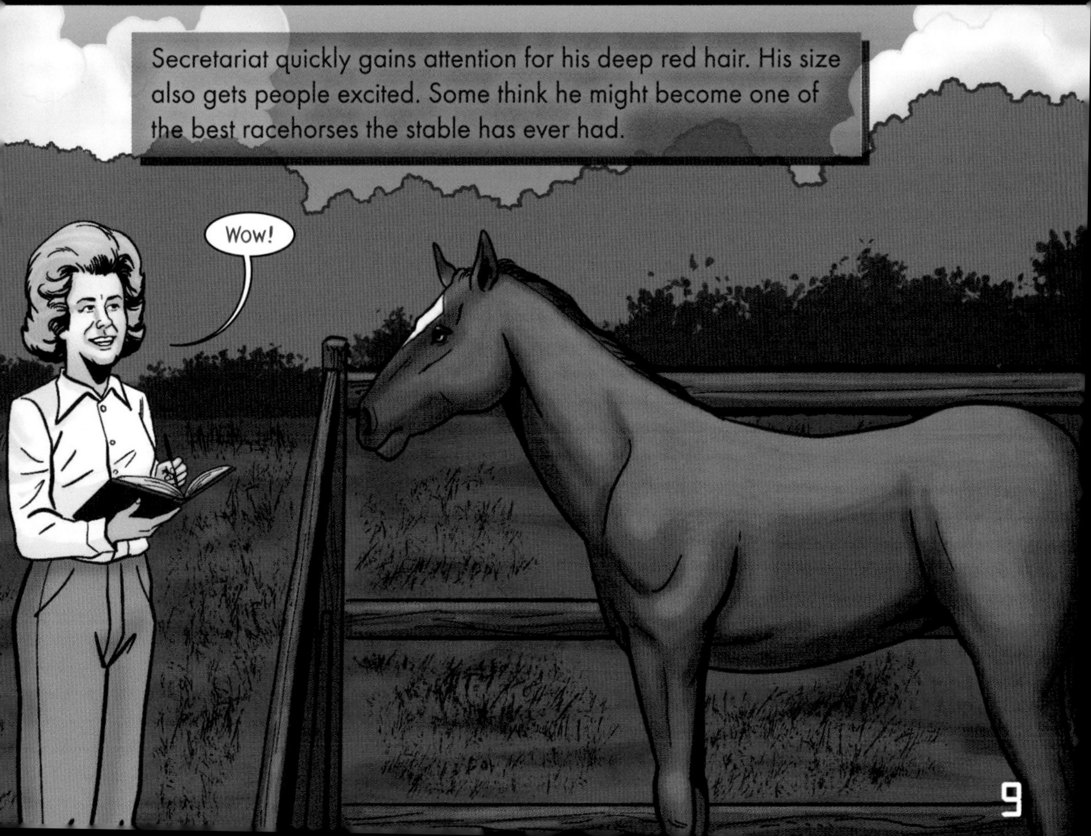
Secretariat quickly gains attention for his deep red hair. His size also gets people excited. Some think he might become one of the best racehorses the stable has ever had.
Wow!

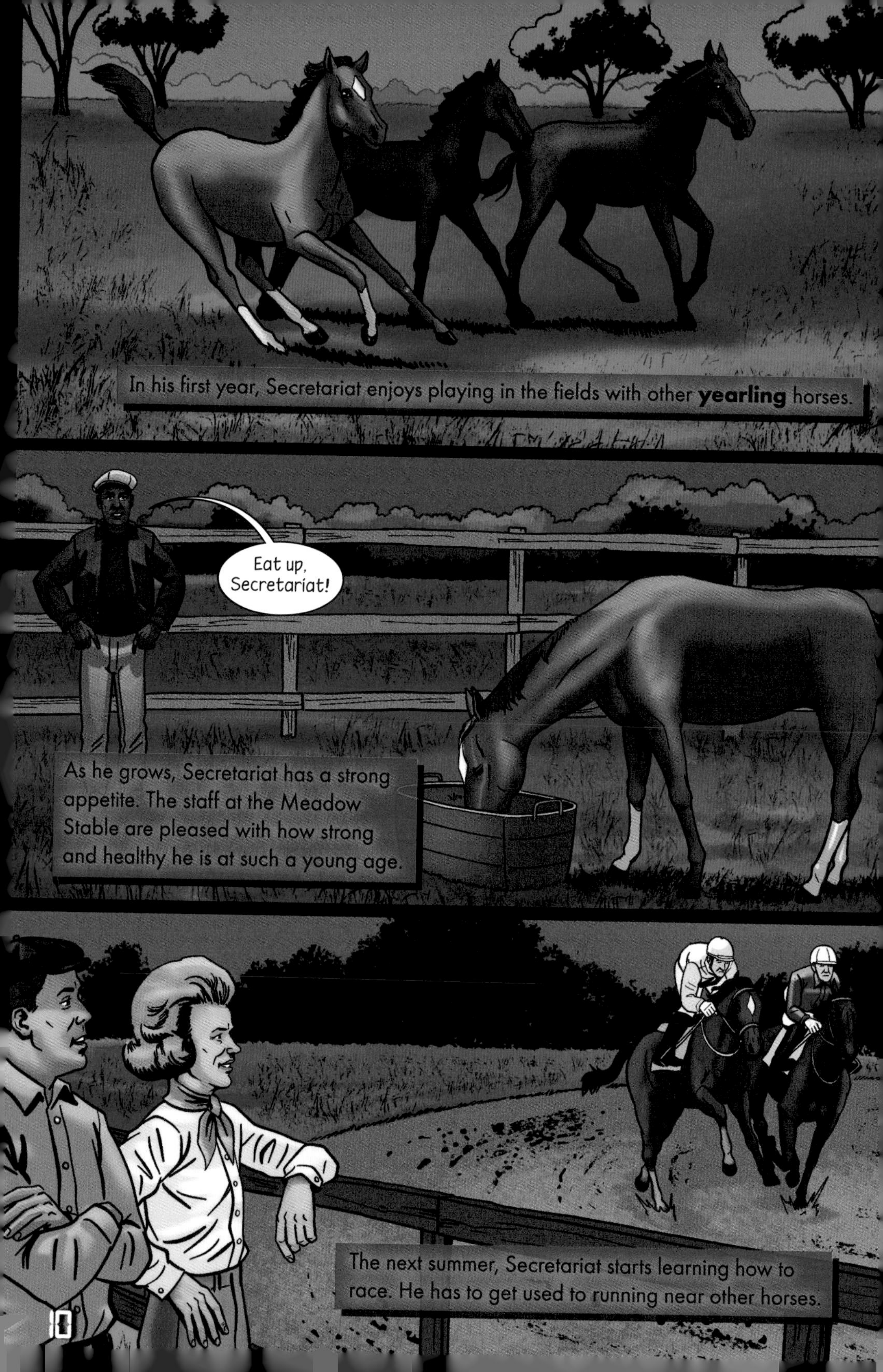
In his first year, Secretariat enjoys playing in the fields with other **yearling** horses.
Eat up, Secretariat!
As he grows, Secretariat has a strong appetite. The staff at the Meadow Stable are pleased with how strong and healthy he is at such a young age.
The next summer, Secretariat starts learning how to race. He has to get used to running near other horses.

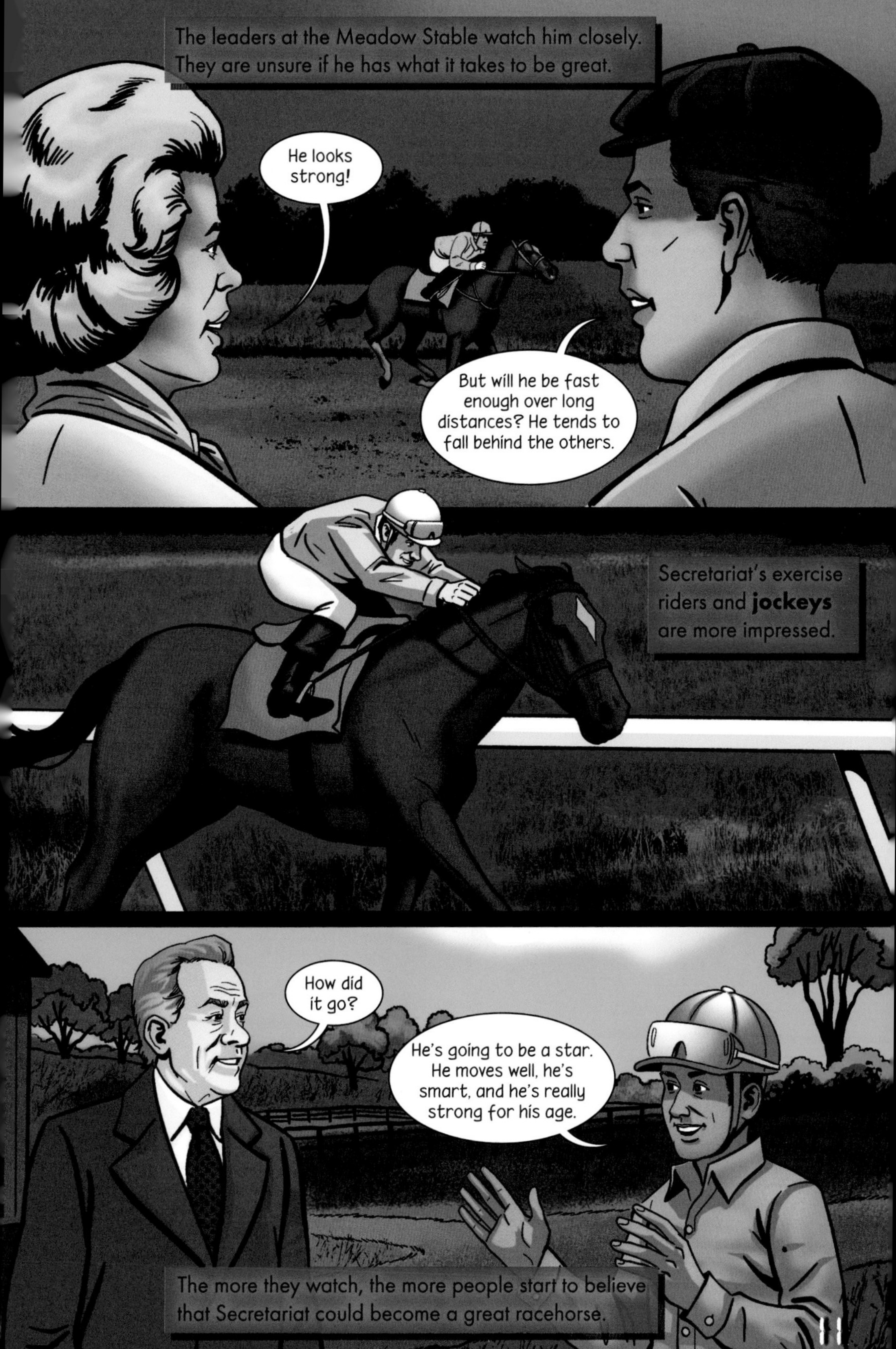
The leaders at the Meadow Stable watch him closely. They are unsure if he has what it takes to be great.
He looks strong!
But will he be fast enough over long distances? He tends to fall behind the others.
Secretariat's exercise riders and **jockeys** are more impressed.
How did it go?
He's going to be a star. He moves well, he's smart, and he's really strong for his age.
The more they watch, the more people start to believe that Secretariat could become a great racehorse.

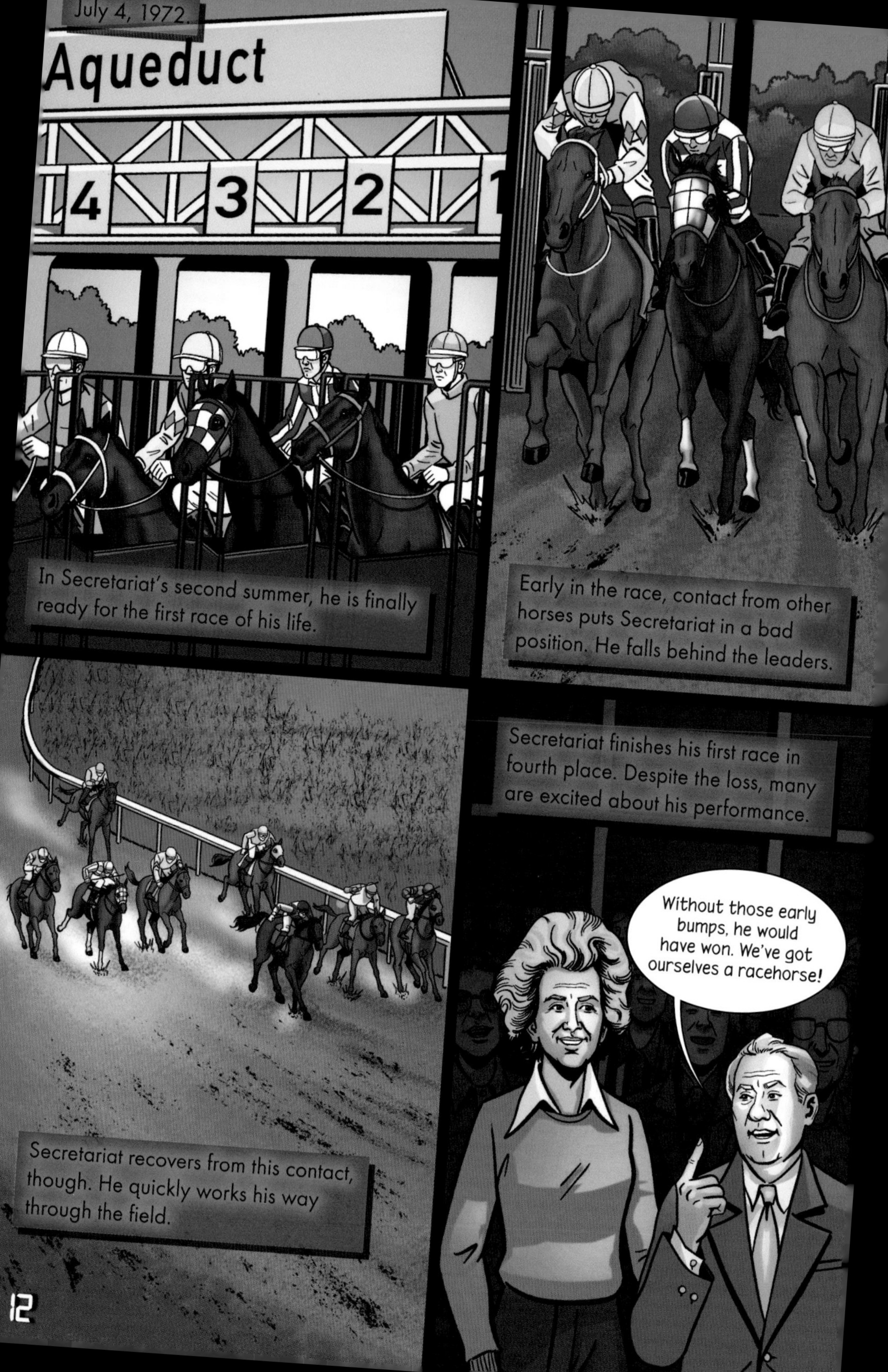
July 4, 1972.
Aqueduct
4
3
2
1
In Secretariat's second summer, he is finally ready for the first race of his life.
Early in the race, contact from other horses puts Secretariat in a bad position. He falls behind the leaders.
Secretariat recovers from this contact, though. He quickly works his way through the field.
Secretariat finishes his first race in fourth place. Despite the loss, many are excited about his performance.
Without those early bumps, he would have won. We've got ourselves a racehorse!

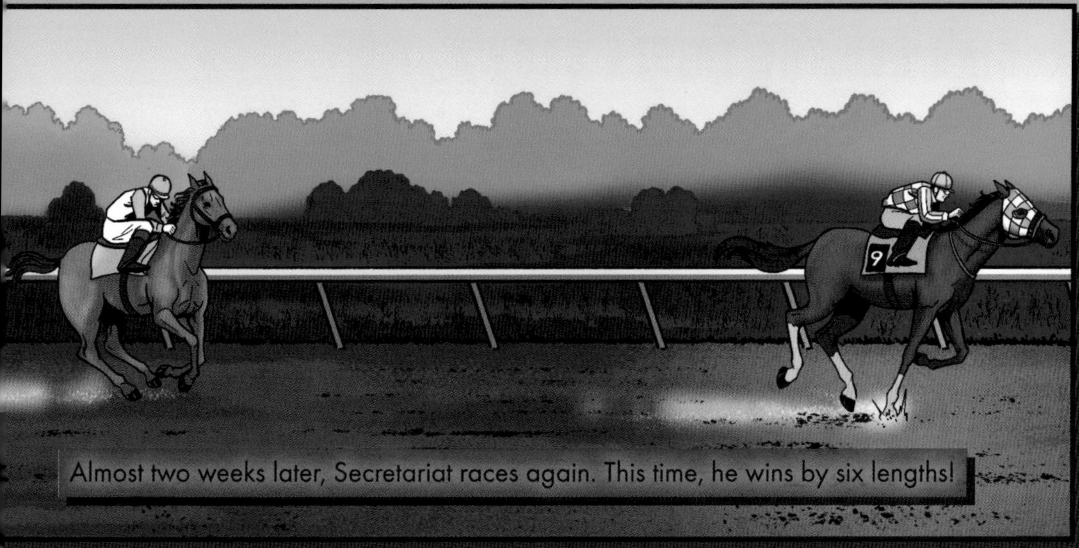
Almost two weeks later, Secretariat races again. This time, he wins by six lengths!

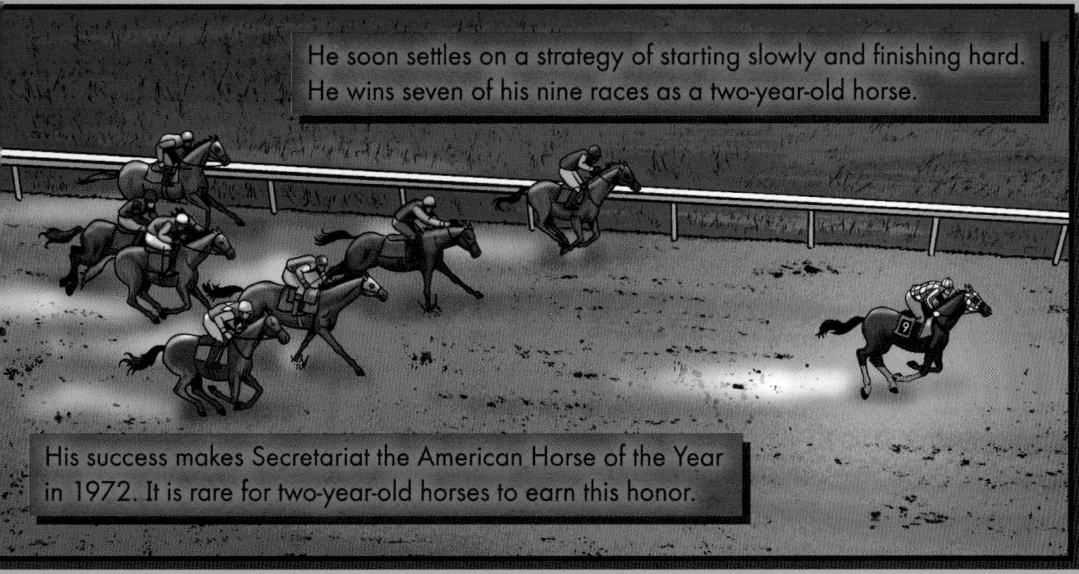
He soon settles on a strategy of starting slowly and finishing hard. He wins seven of his nine races as a two-year-old horse.
His success makes Secretariat the American Horse of the Year in 1972. It is rare for two-year-old horses to earn this honor.

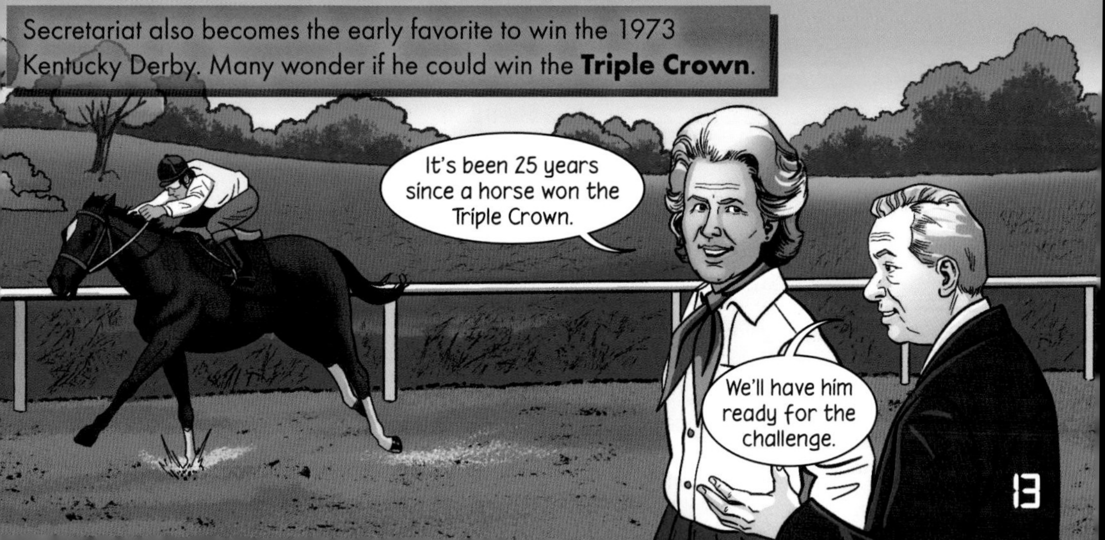
Secretariat also becomes the early favorite to win the 1973 Kentucky Derby. Many wonder if he could win the **Triple Crown**.
It's been 25 years since a horse won the Triple Crown.
We'll have him ready for the challenge.

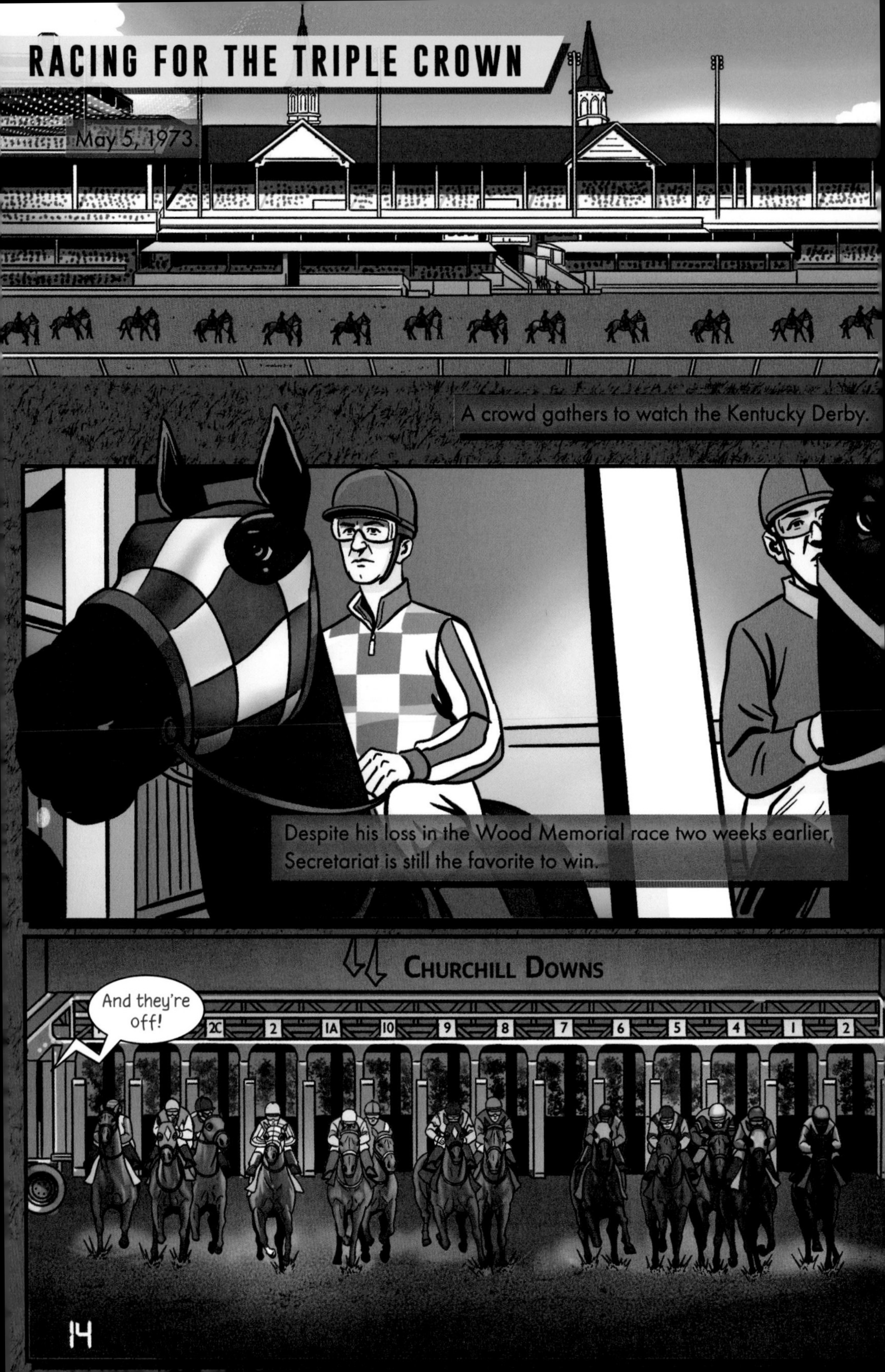
RACING FOR THE TRIPLE CROWN
May 5, 1973.
A crowd gathers to watch the Kentucky Derby.
Despite his loss in the Wood Memorial race two weeks earlier, Secretariat is still the favorite to win.
CHURCHILL DOWNS
And they're off!

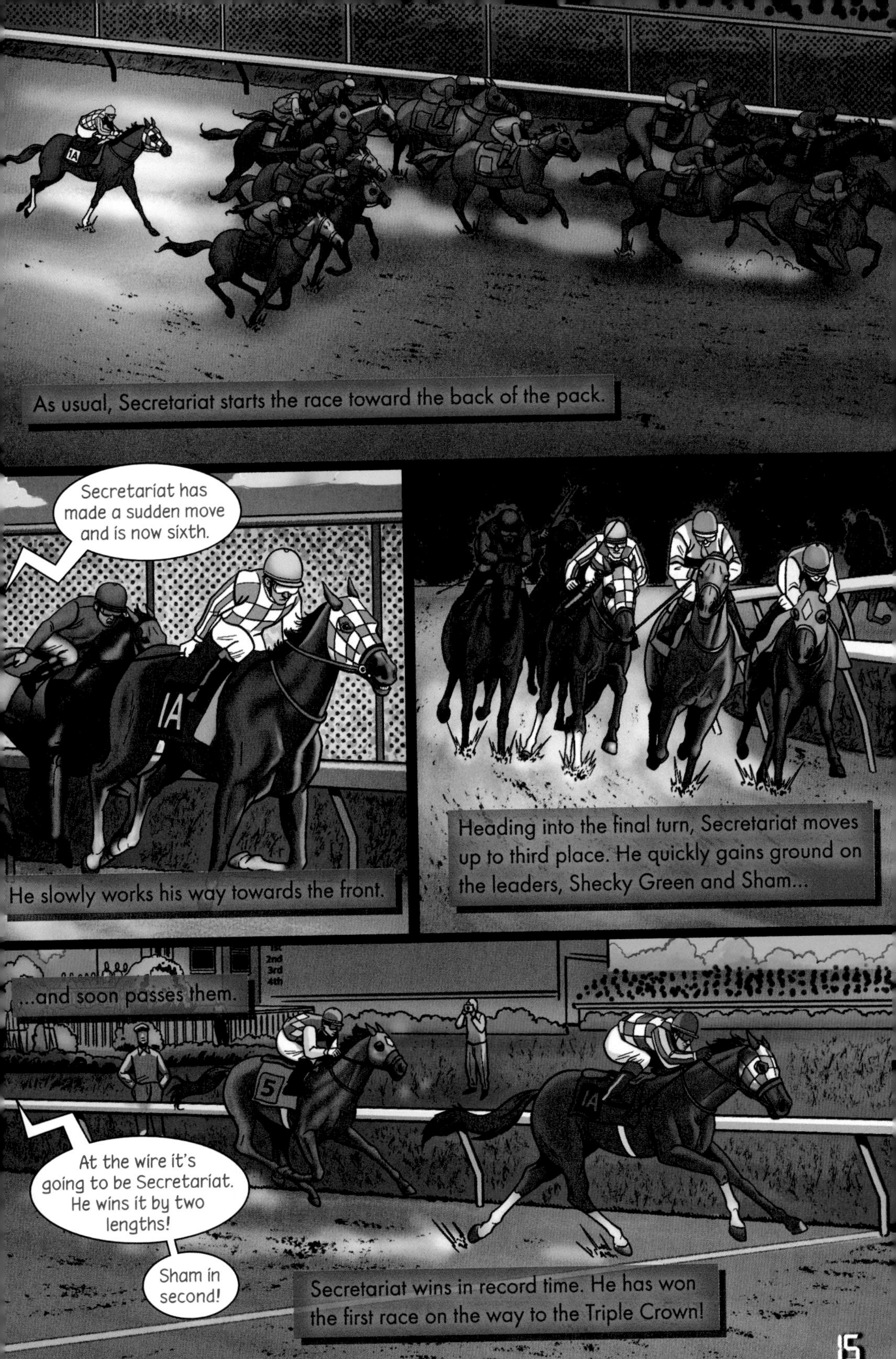
As usual, Secretariat starts the race toward the back of the pack.
Secretariat has made a sudden move and is now sixth.
He slowly works his way towards the front.
Heading into the final turn, Secretariat moves up to third place. He quickly gains ground on the leaders, Shecky Green and Sham...
...and soon passes them.
At the wire it's going to be Secretariat. He wins it by two lengths!
Sham in second!
Secretariat wins in record time. He has won the first race on the way to the Triple Crown!

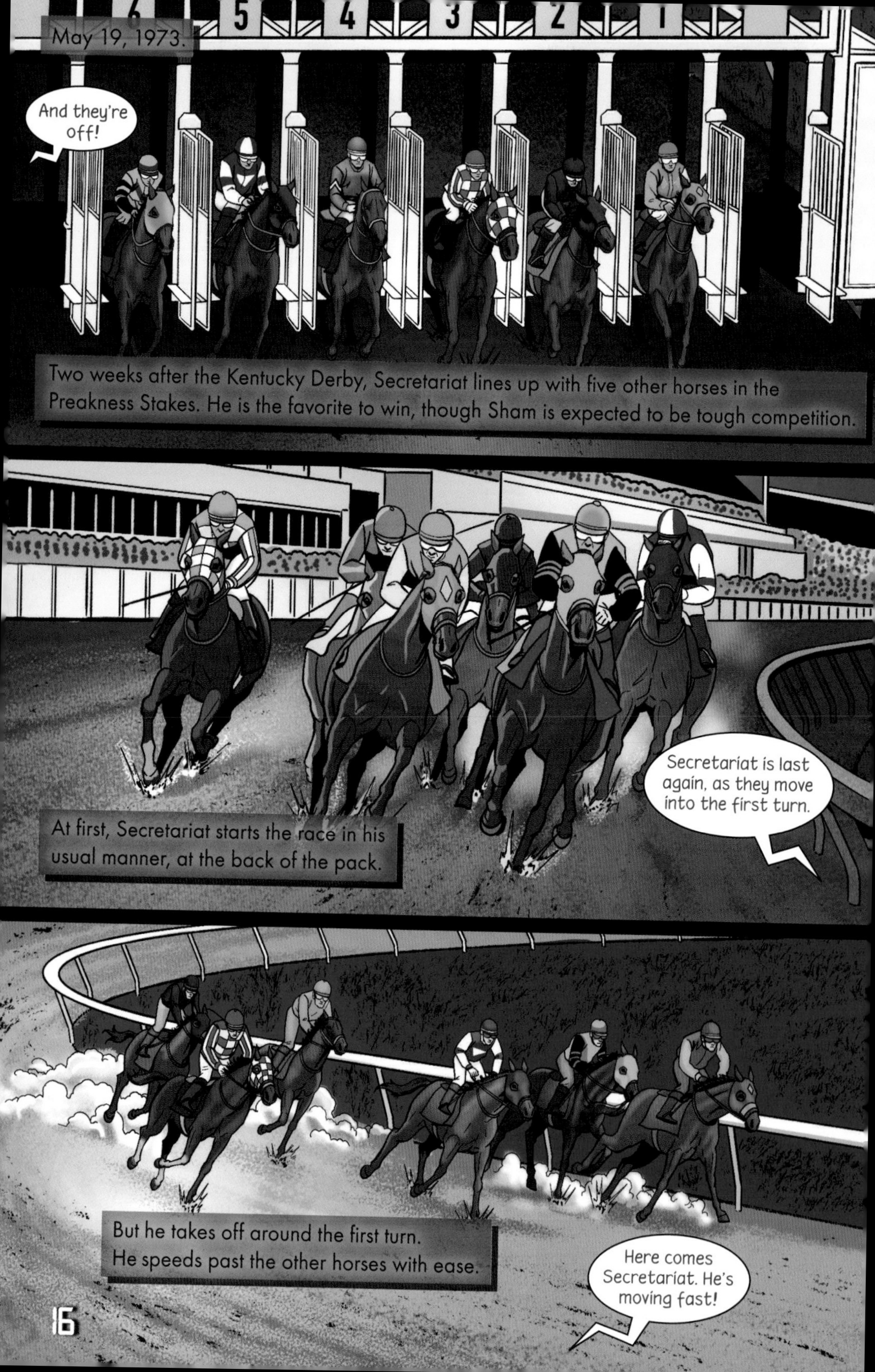
May 19, 1973.
And they're off!
Two weeks after the Kentucky Derby, Secretariat lines up with five other horses in the Preakness Stakes. He is the favorite to win, though Sham is expected to be tough competition.
Secretariat is last again, as they move into the first turn.
At first, Secretariat starts the race in his usual manner, at the back of the pack.
But he takes off around the first turn. He speeds past the other horses with ease.
Here comes Secretariat. He's moving fast!

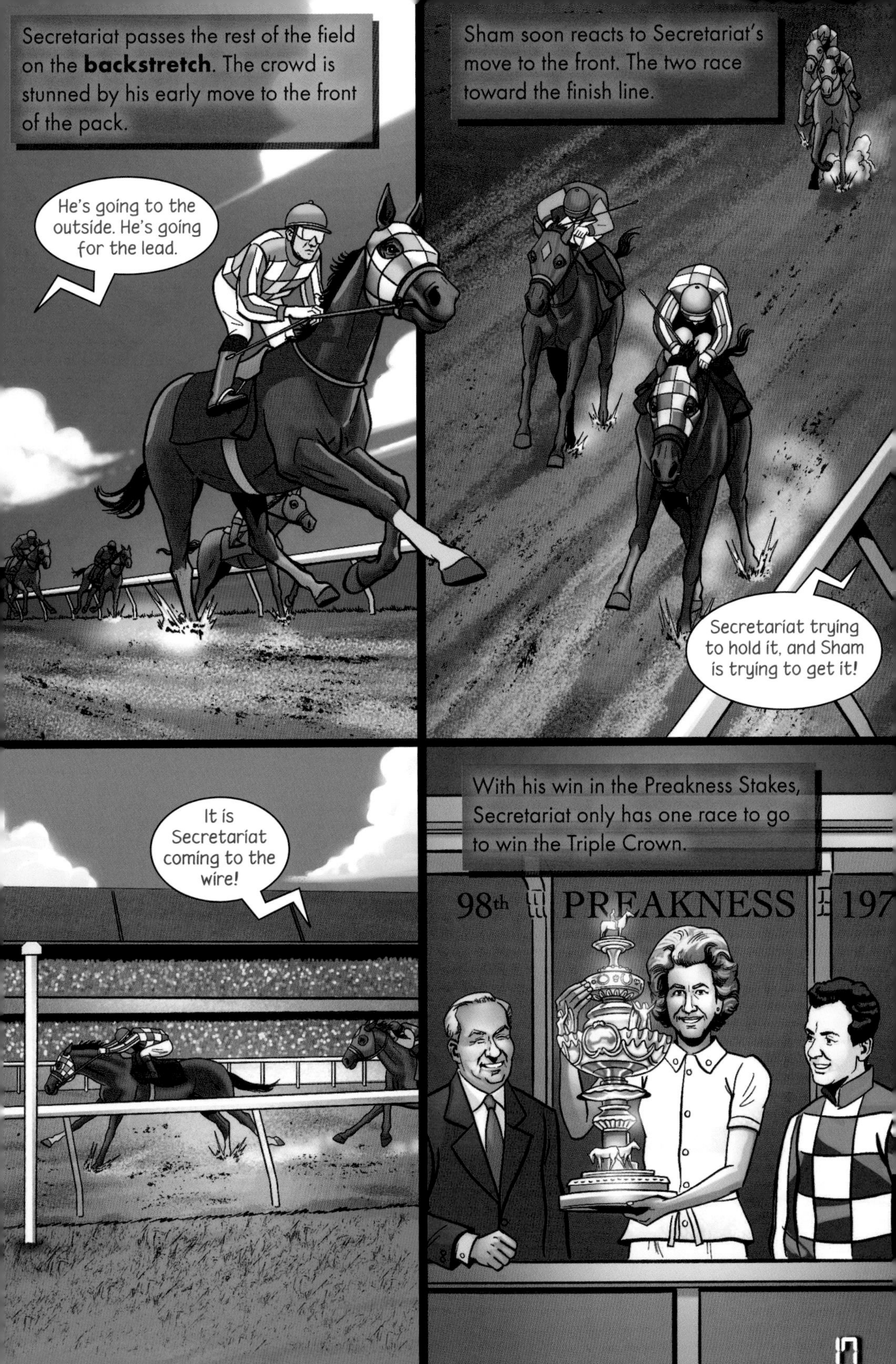
Secretariat passes the rest of the field on the **backstretch**. The crowd is stunned by his early move to the front of the pack.
He's going to the outside. He's going for the lead.
Sham soon reacts to Secretariat's move to the front. The two race toward the finish line.
Secretariat trying to hold it, and Sham is trying to get it!
It is Secretariat coming to the wire!
With his win in the Preakness Stakes, Secretariat only has one race to go to win the Triple Crown.
98th PREAKNESS 197

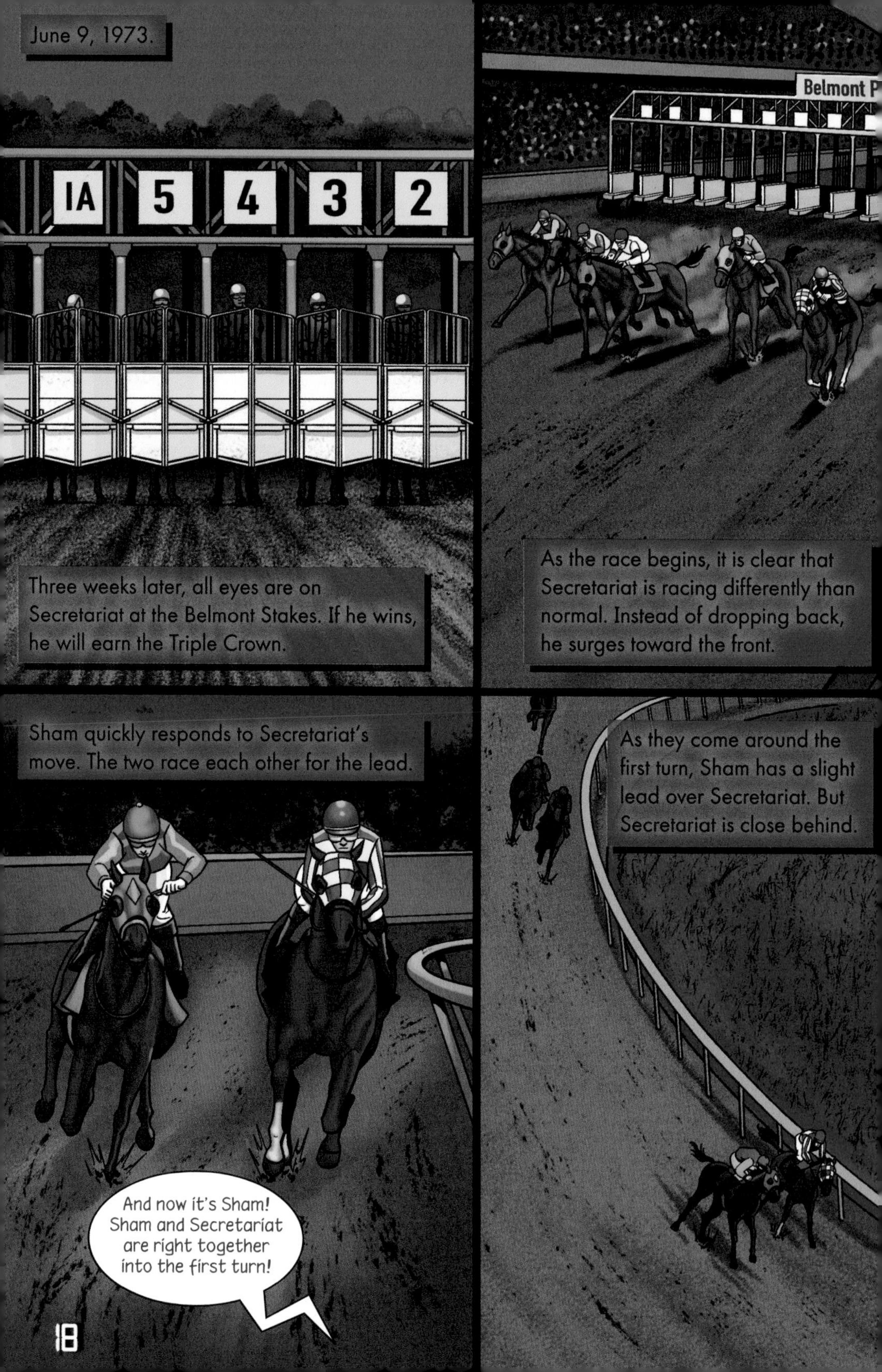
June 9, 1973.
IA 5 4 3 2
Three weeks later, all eyes are on Secretariat at the Belmont Stakes. If he wins, he will earn the Triple Crown.
Belmont P
As the race begins, it is clear that Secretariat is racing differently than normal. Instead of dropping back, he surges toward the front.
Sham quickly responds to Secretariat's move. The two race each other for the lead.
And now it's Sham! Sham and Secretariat are right together into the first turn!
As they come around the first turn, Sham has a slight lead over Secretariat. But Secretariat is close behind.

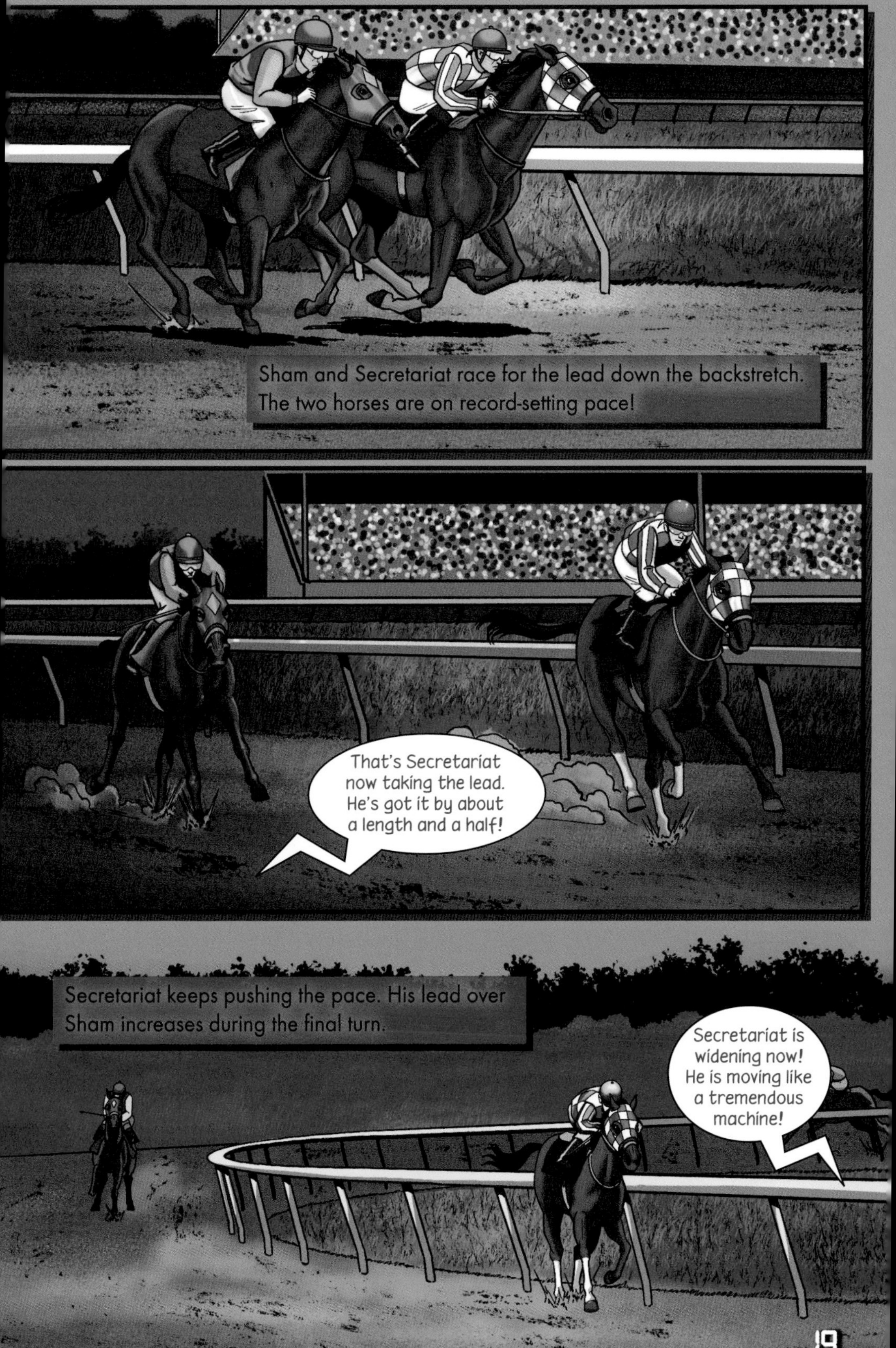
Sham and Secretariat race for the lead down the backstretch. The two horses are on record-setting pace!
That's Secretariat now taking the lead. He's got it by about a length and a half!
Secretariat keeps pushing the pace. His lead over Sham increases during the final turn.
Secretariat is widening now! He is moving like a tremendous machine!

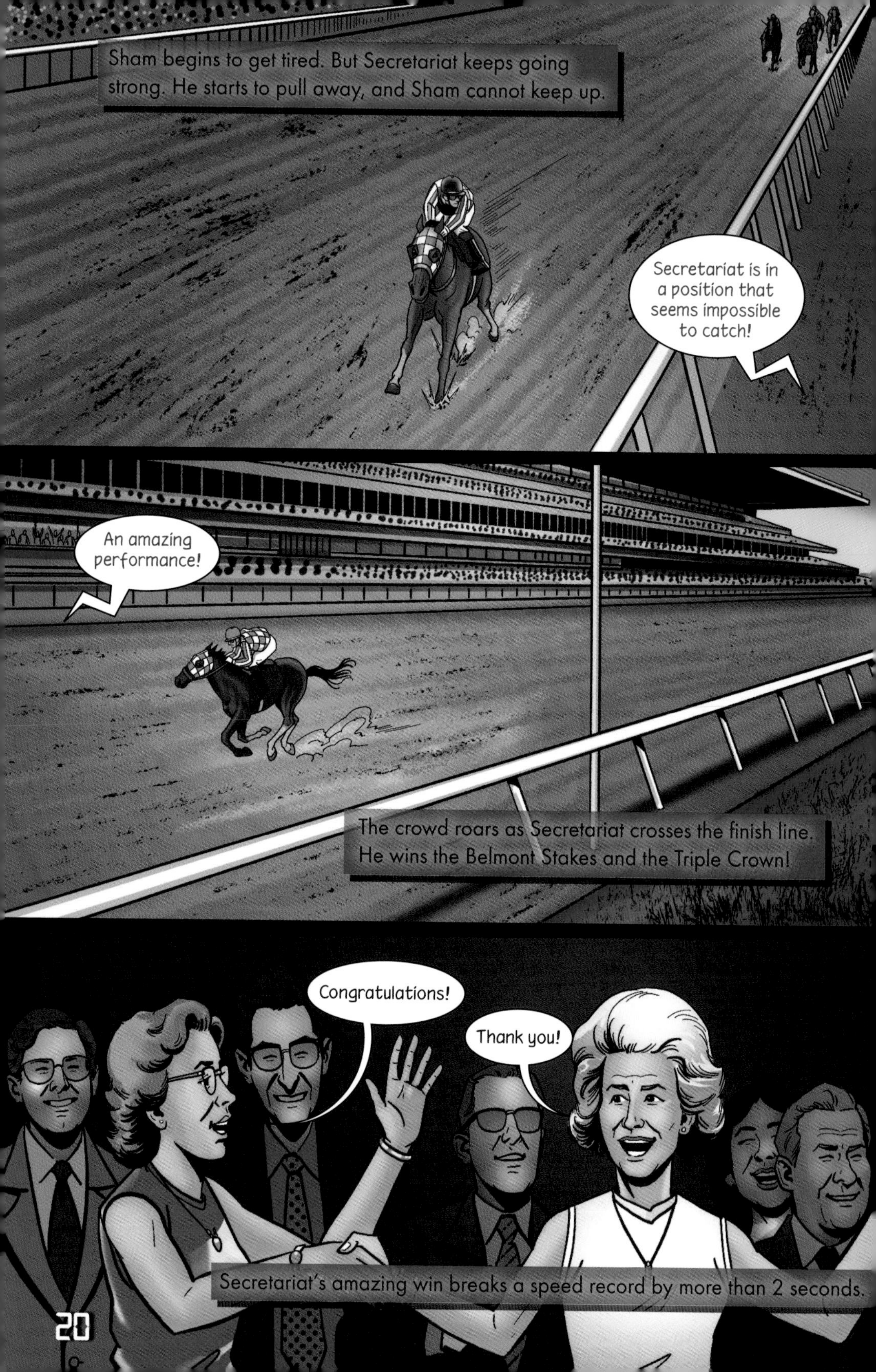

Sham begins to get tired. But Secretariat keeps going strong. He starts to pull away, and Sham cannot keep up.
Secretariat is in a position that seems impossible to catch!
An amazing performance!
The crowd roars as Secretariat crosses the finish line. He wins the Belmont Stakes and the Triple Crown!
Congratulations!
Thank you!
Secretariat's amazing win breaks a speed record by more than 2 seconds.

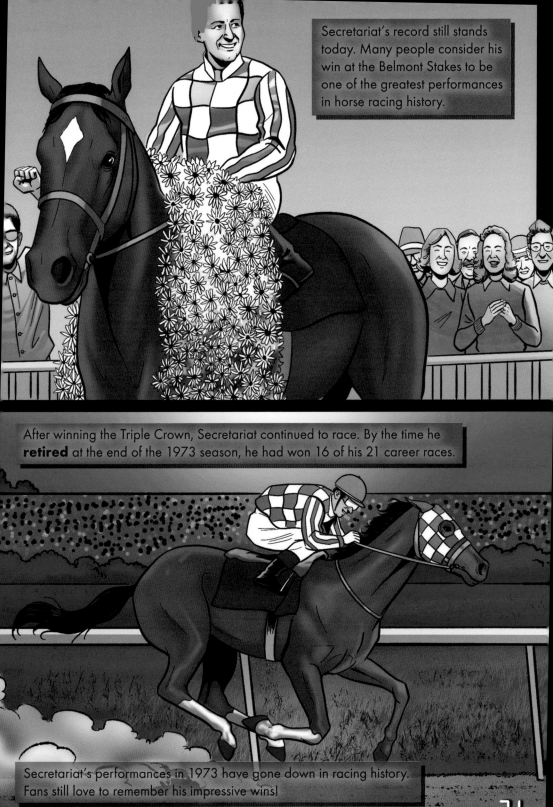

Secretariat's record still stands today. Many people consider his win at the Belmont Stakes to be one of the greatest performances in horse racing history.

After winning the Triple Crown, Secretariat continued to race. By the time he **retired** at the end of the 1973 season, he had won 16 of his 21 career races.

Secretariat's performances in 1973 have gone down in racing history. Fans still love to remember his impressive wins!

MORE ABOUT SECRETARIAT

- Secretariat was named American Horse of the Year in 1972 and 1973.

- He was inducted into the National Museum of Racing and Hall of Fame in 1974.

- Secretariat broke records in all three of the Triple Crown races that he won.

- His time in the Belmont Stakes is still the American record for 1.5 miles on a dirt track.

SECRETARIAT TIMELINE

MARCH 30, 1970
Secretariat is born at the Meadow Stable

MAY 19, 1973
Secretariat makes an early move to win the Preakness Stakes

NOVEMBER 1973
Secretariat retires from racing

MAY 5, 1973
Secretariat has a late surge to win the Kentucky Derby

JUNE 9, 1973
Secretariat runs away from the field to win the Belmont Stakes and the Triple Crown

BELMONT STAKES
ELMONT, NEW YORK

PREAKNESS STAKES
BALTIMORE, MARYLAND

KENTUCKY DERBY
LOUISVILLE, KENTUCKY

MEADOW STABLE
DOSWELL, VIRGINIA

GLOSSARY

backstretch—the part of a racecourse that is furthest from the viewers

bred—mated to produce a foal

colt—a young male horse

filly—a young female horse

foals—newborn horses

jockeys—people who ride horses during races

retired—stopped racing competitively

sires—male parents of young horses

Triple Crown—an honor for winning three important horse races in one season; the Triple Crown includes the Kentucky Derby, the Preakness Stakes, and the Belmont Stakes.

yearling—a horse that is less than two years old

TO LEARN MORE

AT THE LIBRARY

Dell, Pamela. *Thoroughbreds*. New York, N.Y.: AV2, 2019.

Gitlin, Martin. *Ticket to the Triple Crown*. Ann Arbor, Mich.: Cherry Lake Publishing, 2023.

Klepeis, Alicia Z. *Kentucky*. Minneapolis, Minn.: Bellwether Media, 2022.

ON THE WEB

FACTSURFER

Factsurfer.com gives you a safe, fun way to find more information.

1. Go to www.factsurfer.com
2. Enter "Secretariat" into the search box and click 🔍.
3. Select your book cover to see a list of related content.

INDEX

MEDICAL BREAKTHROUGHS

INCUBATORS

A GRAPHIC HISTORY

PAIGE V. POLINSKY

ILLUSTRATED BY JOSEP RURAL

GRAPHIC UNIVERSE™ • MINNEAPOLIS

Graphic Universe™
An imprint of Lerner Publishing Group, Inc.
241 First Avenue North
Minneapolis, MN 55401 USA

For reading levels and more information, look up this title at www.lernerbooks.com.

Main body text is set in Dave Gibbons Lower. Typeface provided by Comicraft.

Library of Congress Cataloging-in-Publication Data

Names: Polinsky, Paige V., author. | Rural, Josep, illustrator.
Title: Incubators : a graphic history / Paige V. Polinsky ; illustrations by Josep Rural.
Description: Minneapolis : Graphic Universe , [2022] | Series: Medical breakthroughs |
    Includes bibliographical references and index. | Audience: Ages 8–12 | Audience:
    Grades 4–6 | Summary: "When a baby is born early, an incubator helps the child
    keep growing. At first, some medical experts were skeptical about these special
    cribs. But trailblazing doctors' "incubator exhibits" showed people how incubators
    save lives"— Provided by publisher.
Identifiers: LCCN 2021014435 (print) | LCCN 2021014436 (ebook) | ISBN 9781541581517
    (library binding) | ISBN 9781728448718 (paperback) | ISBN 9781728444116 (ebook)
Subjects: LCSH: Incubators (Pediatrics)—Juvenile literature. | Premature infants—Juvenile
    literature.
Classification: LCC RJ34.5.I52 P65 2022 (print) | LCC RJ34.5.I52 (ebook) | DDC
    618.92/011—dc23

LC record available at https://lccn.loc.gov/2021014435
LC ebook record available at https://lccn.loc.gov/2021014436

Manufactured in the United States of America
1 – CG – 12/15/21

TABLE OF CONTENTS

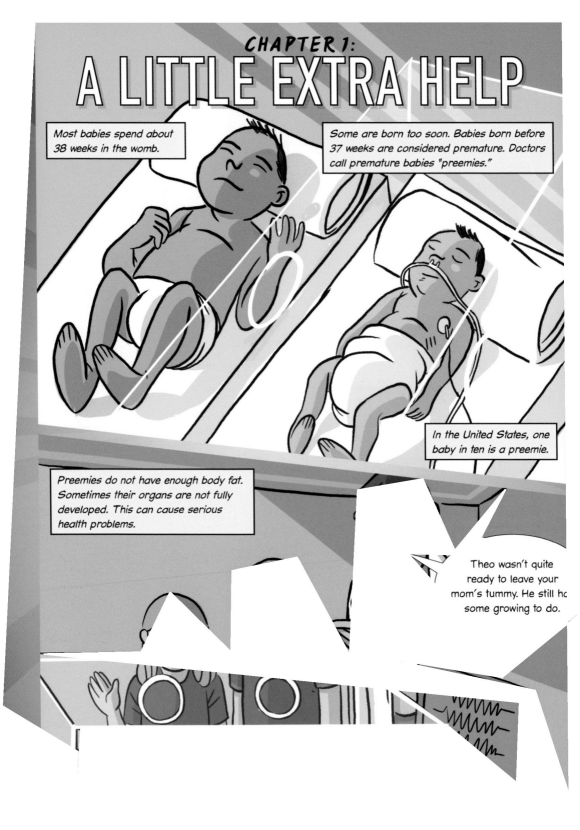

CHAPTER 1:
A LITTLE EXTRA HELP

Most babies spend about 38 weeks in the womb.

Some are born too soon. Babies born before 37 weeks are considered premature. Doctors call premature babies "preemies."

In the United States, one baby in ten is a preemie.

Preemies do not have enough body fat. Sometimes their organs are not fully developed. This can cause serious health problems.

Theo wasn't quite ready to leave your mom's tummy. He still ha[s] some growing to do.

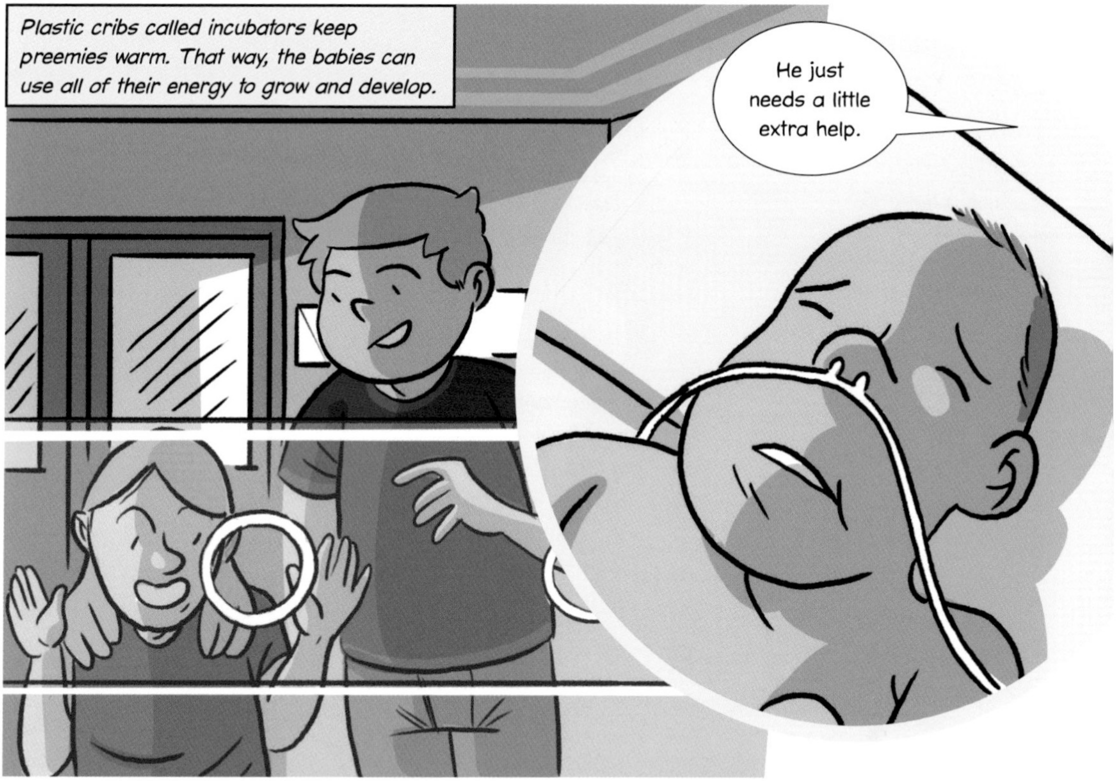
Plastic cribs called incubators keep preemies warm. That way, the babies can use all of their energy to grow and develop.
He just needs a little extra help.

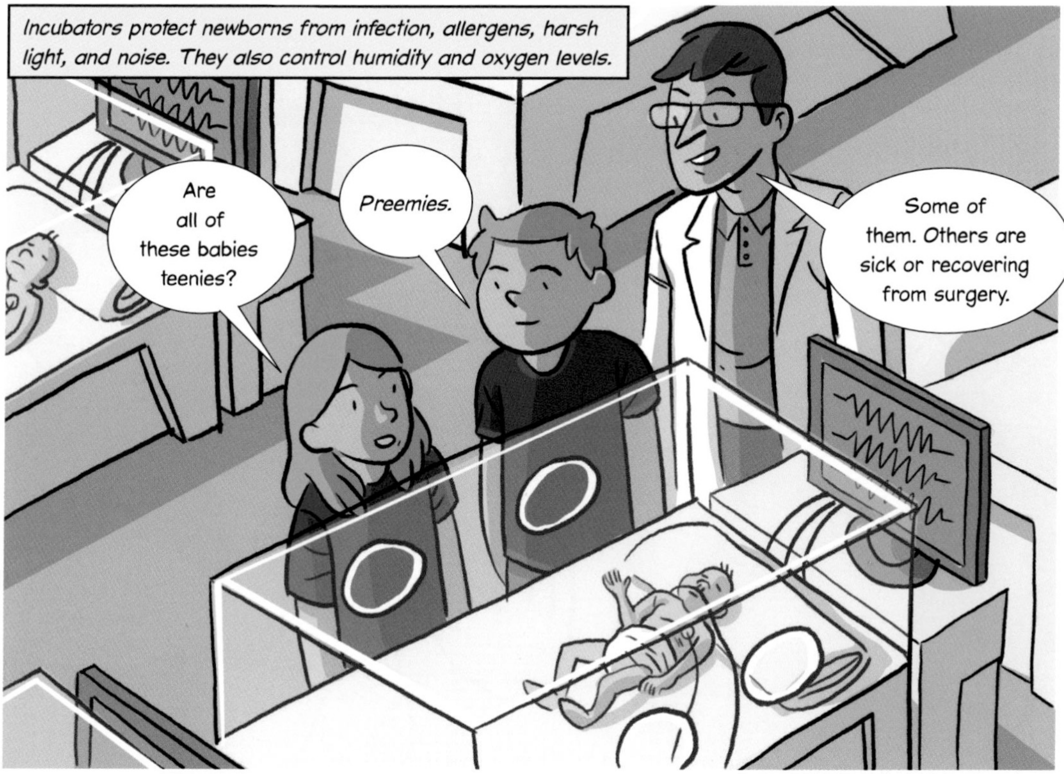
Incubators protect newborns from infection, allergens, harsh light, and noise. They also control humidity and oxygen levels.
Are all of these babies teenies?
Preemies.
Some of them. Others are sick or recovering from surgery.

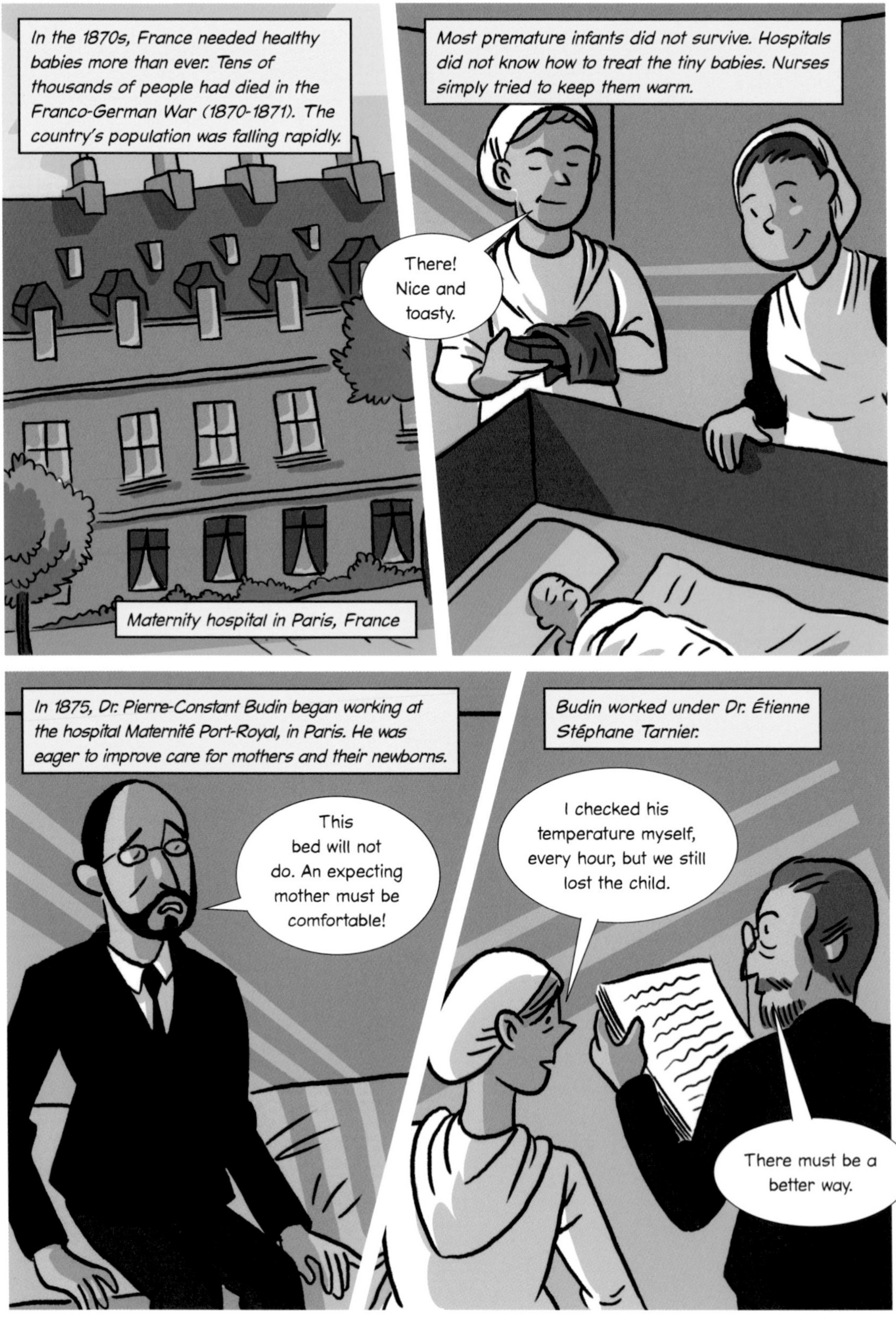
In the 1870s, France needed healthy babies more than ever. Tens of thousands of people had died in the Franco-German War (1870-1871). The country's population was falling rapidly.
Maternity hospital in Paris, France
Most premature infants did not survive. Hospitals did not know how to treat the tiny babies. Nurses simply tried to keep them warm.
There! Nice and toasty.
In 1875, Dr. Pierre-Constant Budin began working at the hospital Maternité Port-Royal, in Paris. He was eager to improve care for mothers and their newborns.
This bed will not do. An expecting mother must be comfortable!
Budin worked under Dr. Étienne Stéphane Tarnier.
I checked his temperature myself, every hour, but we still lost the child.
There must be a better way.

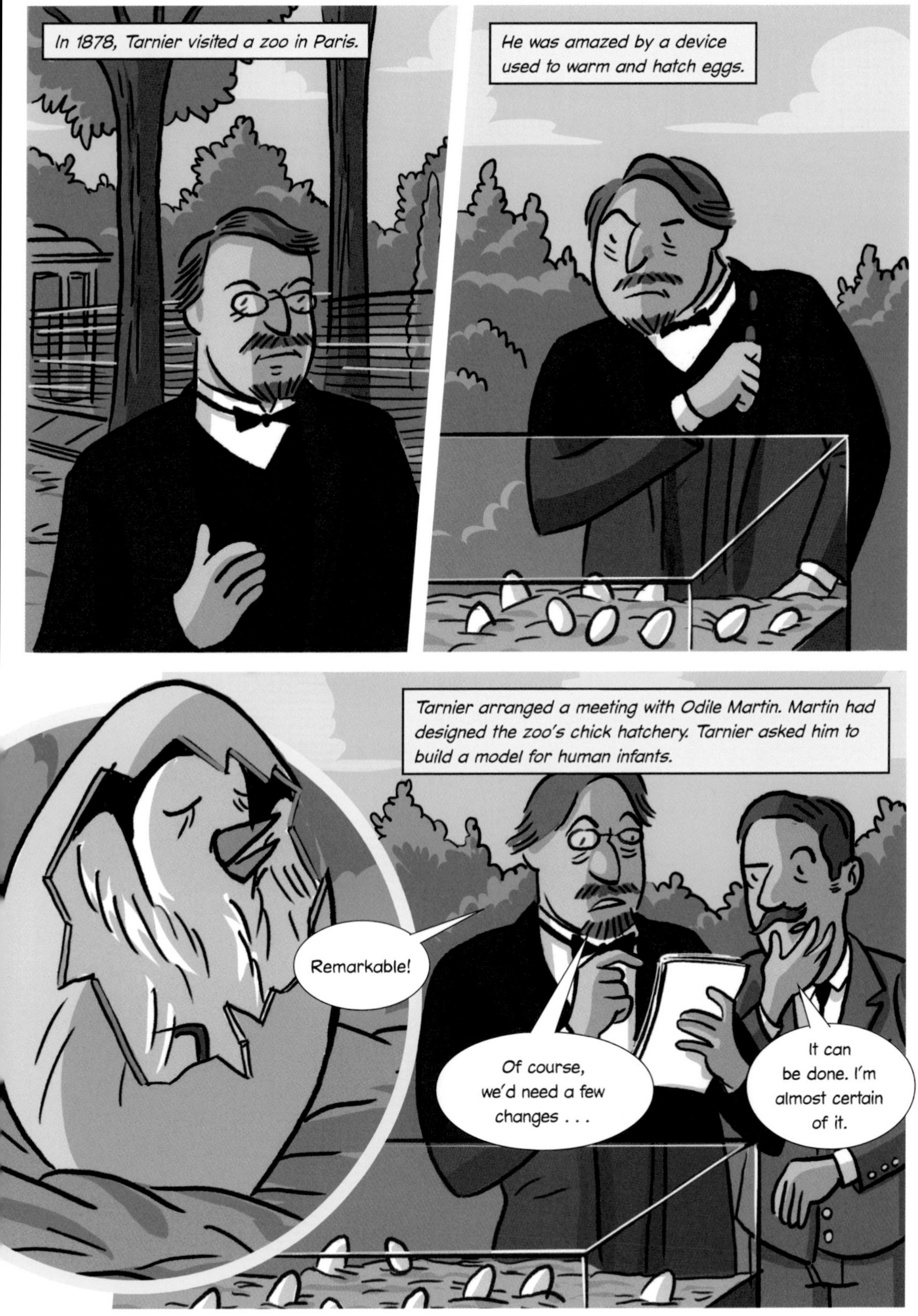
In 1878, Tarnier visited a zoo in Paris.
He was amazed by a device used to warm and hatch eggs.
Tarnier arranged a meeting with Odile Martin. Martin had designed the zoo's chick hatchery. Tarnier asked him to build a model for human infants.
Remarkable!
Of course, we'd need a few changes . . .
It can be done. I'm almost certain of it.

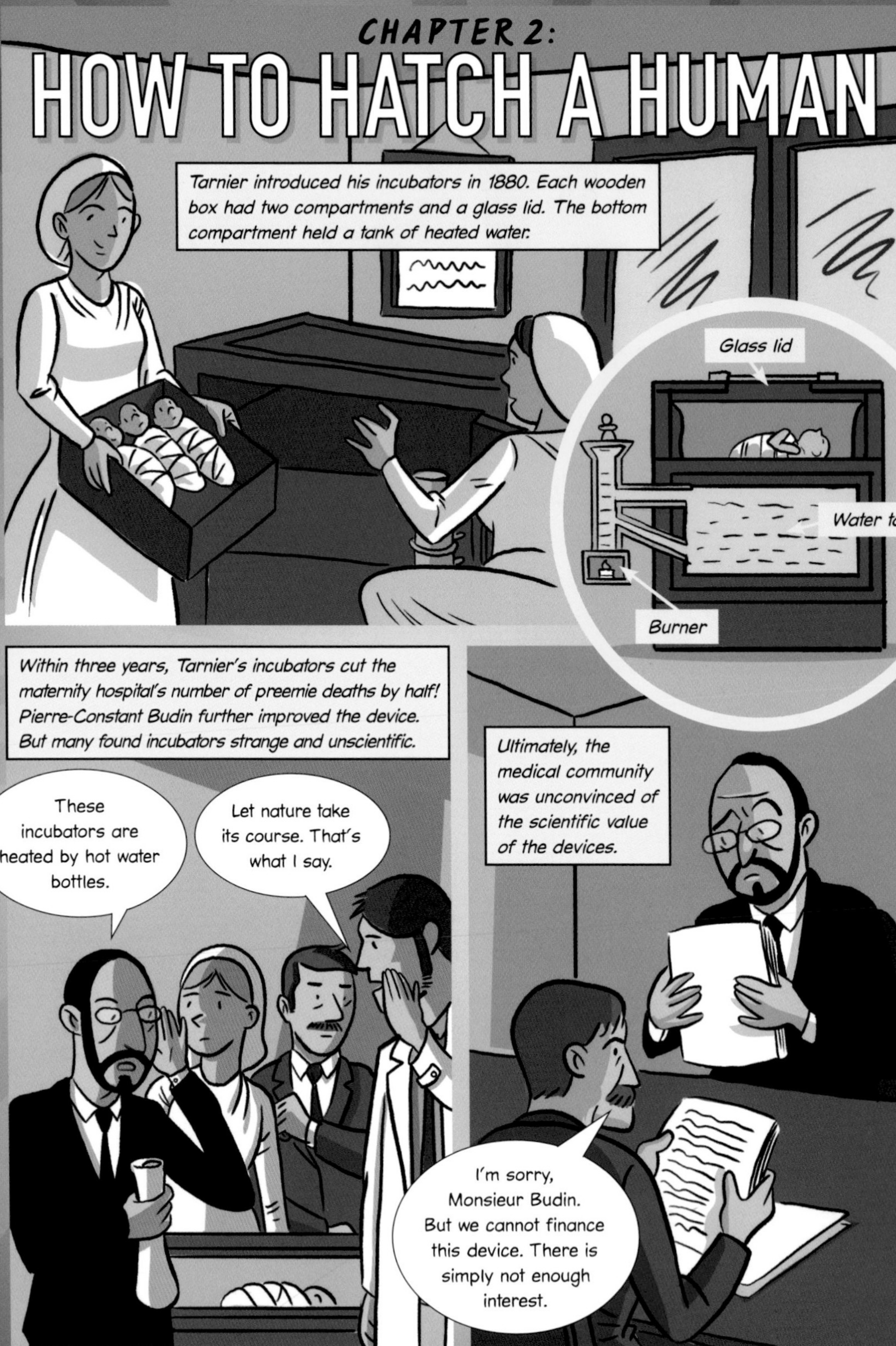
CHAPTER 2:
HOW TO HATCH A HUMAN
Tarnier introduced his incubators in 1880. Each wooden box had two compartments and a glass lid. The bottom compartment held a tank of heated water.
Glass lid
Water tank
Burner
Within three years, Tarnier's incubators cut the maternity hospital's number of preemie deaths by half! Pierre-Constant Budin further improved the device. But many found incubators strange and unscientific.
These incubators are heated by hot water bottles.
Let nature take its course. That's what I say.
Ultimately, the medical community was unconvinced of the scientific value of the devices.
I'm sorry, Monsieur Budin. But we cannot finance this device. There is simply not enough interest.

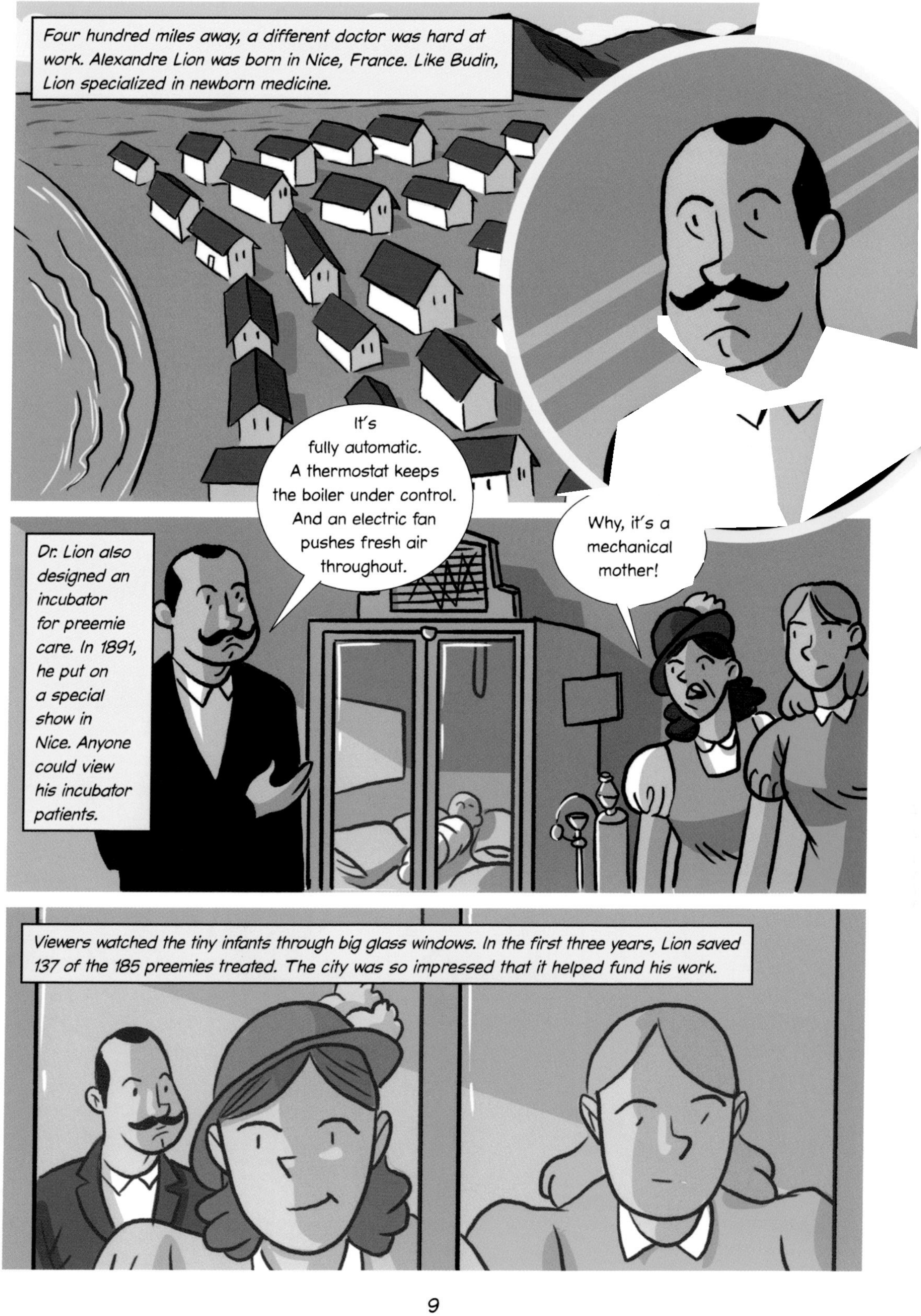
Four hundred miles away, a different doctor was hard at work. Alexandre Lion was born in Nice, France. Like Budin, Lion specialized in newborn medicine.
Dr. Lion also designed an incubator for preemie care. In 1891, he put on a special show in Nice. Anyone could view his incubator patients.
It's fully automatic. A thermostat keeps the boiler under control. And an electric fan pushes fresh air throughout.
Why, it's a mechanical mother!
Viewers watched the tiny infants through big glass windows. In the first three years, Lion saved 137 of the 185 preemies treated. The city was so impressed that it helped fund his work.

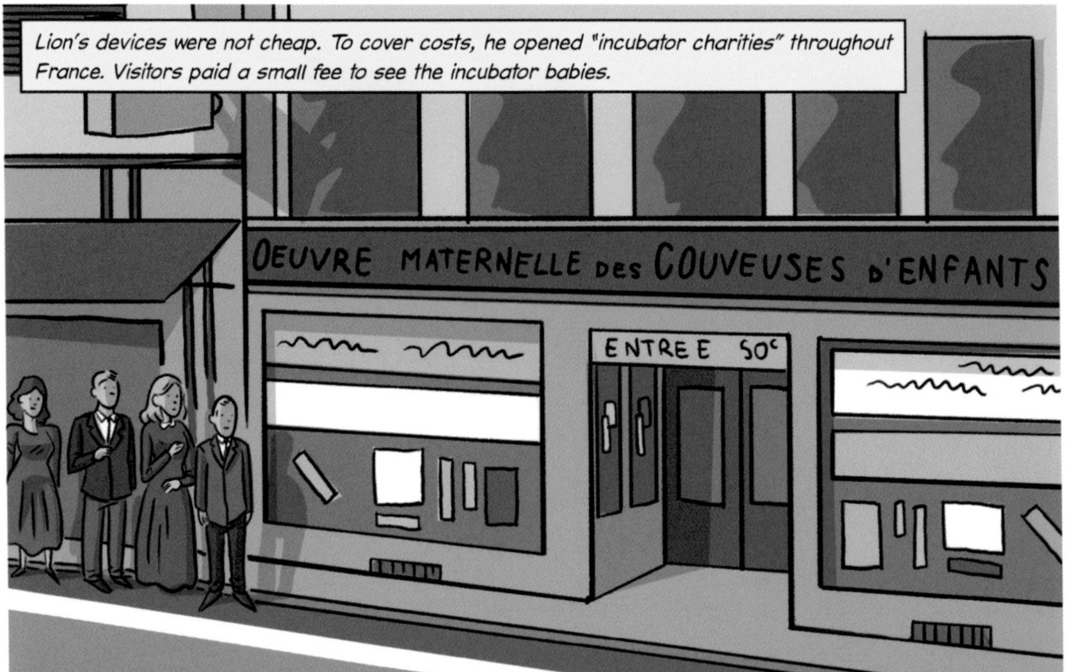
Lion's devices were not cheap. To cover costs, he opened "incubator charities" throughout France. Visitors paid a small fee to see the incubator babies.
OEUVRE MATERNELLE des COUVEUSES D'ENFANTS
ENTREE 50c

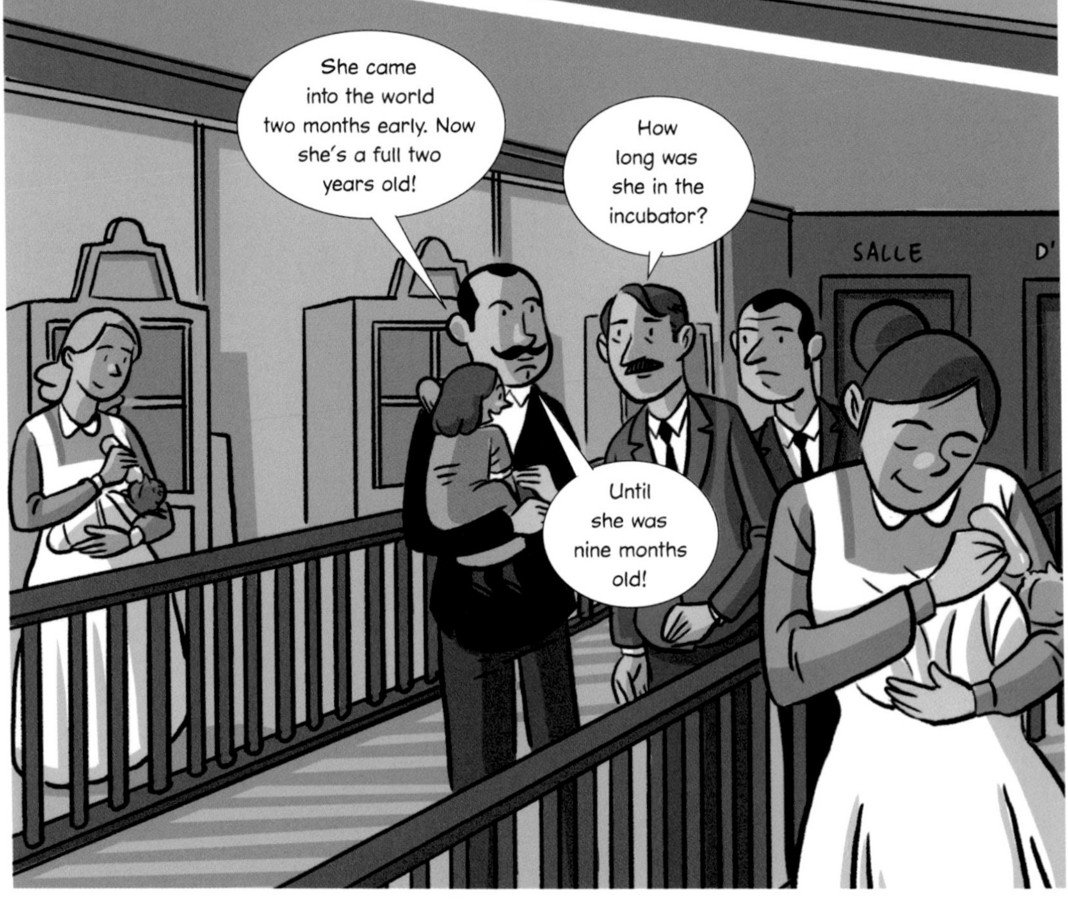
She came into the world two months early. Now she's a full two years old!
How long was she in the incubator?
Until she was nine months old!
SALLE

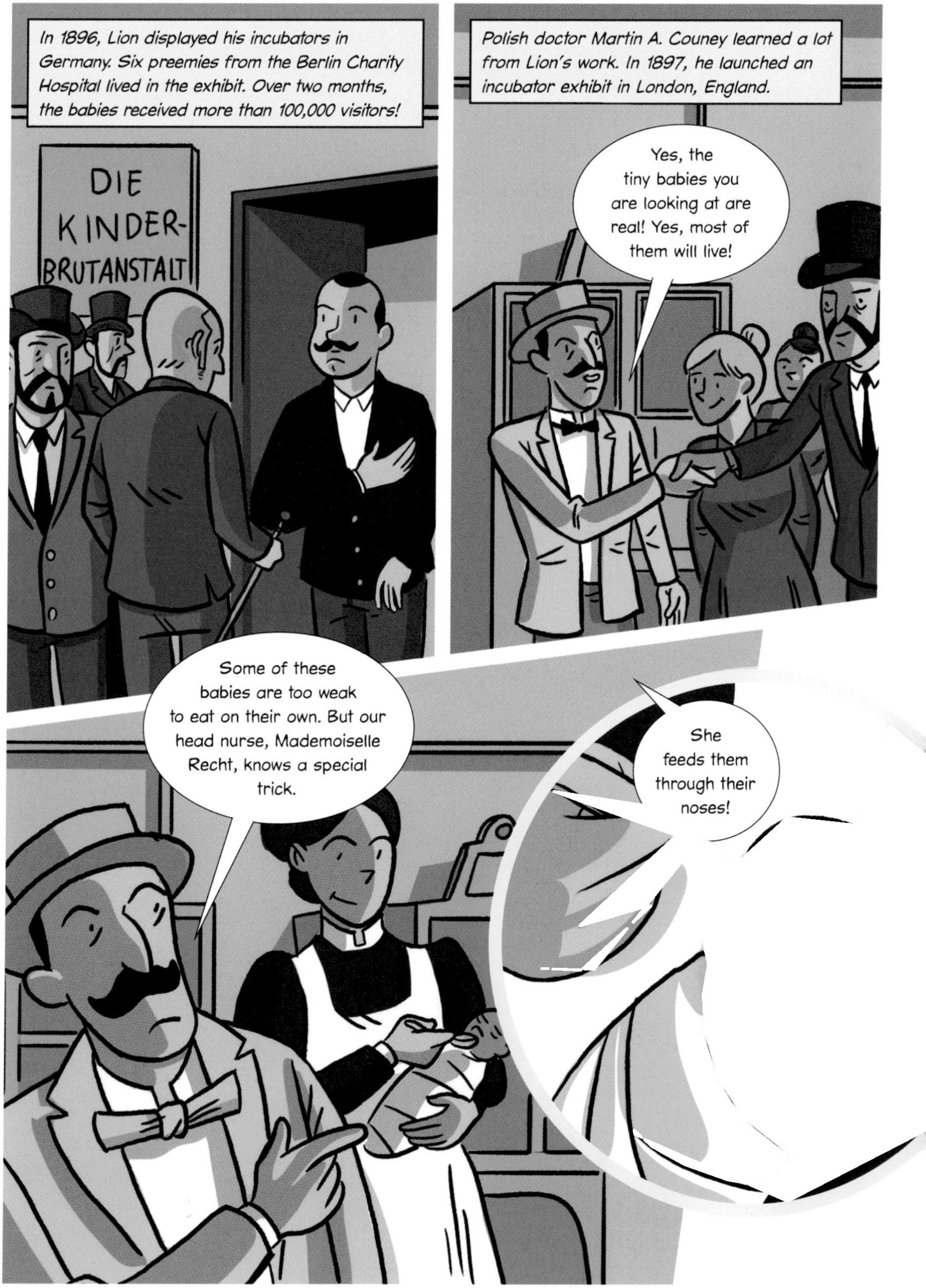
In 1896, Lion displayed his incubators in Germany. Six preemies from the Berlin Charity Hospital lived in the exhibit. Over two months, the babies received more than 100,000 visitors!
DIE KINDER-BRUTANSTALT
Polish doctor Martin A. Couney learned a lot from Lion's work. In 1897, he launched an incubator exhibit in London, England.
Yes, the tiny babies you are looking at are real! Yes, most of them will live!
Some of these babies are too weak to eat on their own. But our head nurse, Mademoiselle Recht, knows a special trick.
She feeds them through their noses!

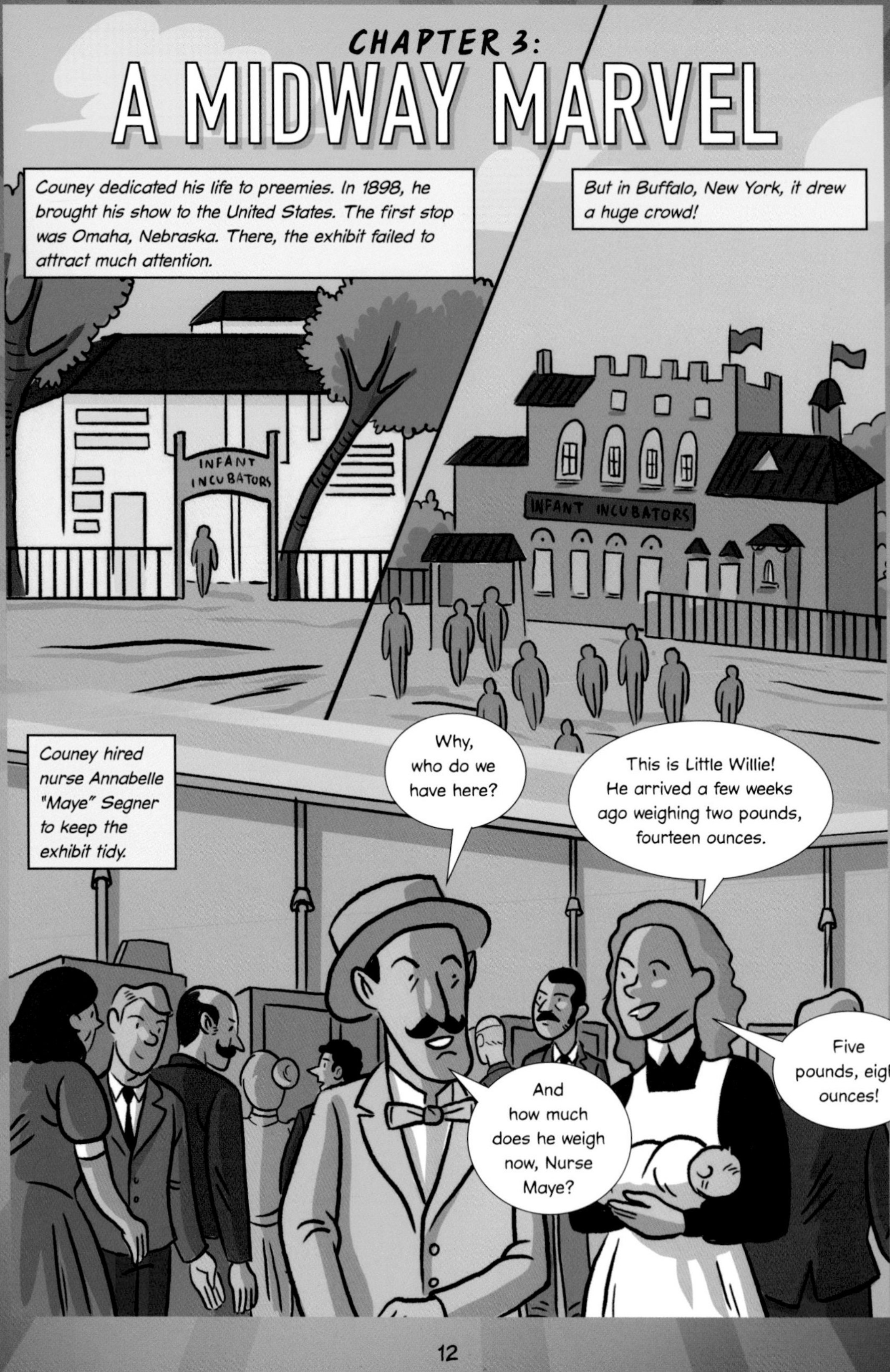
CHAPTER 3:
A MIDWAY MARVEL
Couney dedicated his life to preemies. In 1898, he brought his show to the United States. The first stop was Omaha, Nebraska. There, the exhibit failed to attract much attention.
INFANT INCUBATORS
But in Buffalo, New York, it drew a huge crowd!
INFANT INCUBATORS
Couney hired nurse Annabelle "Maye" Segner to keep the exhibit tidy.
Why, who do we have here?
This is Little Willie! He arrived a few weeks ago weighing two pounds, fourteen ounces.
And how much does he weigh now, Nurse Maye?
Five pounds, eight ounces!

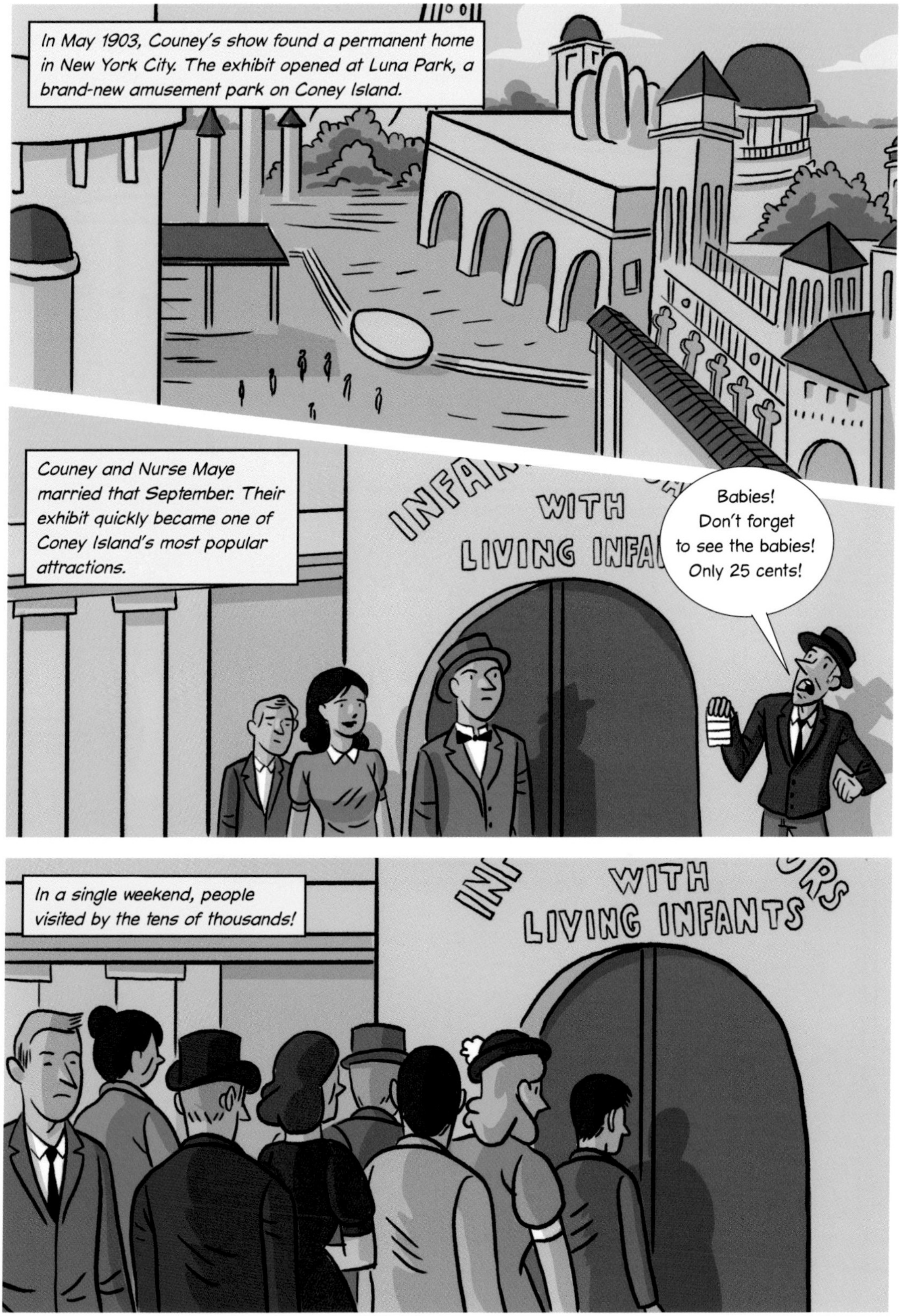
In May 1903, Couney's show found a permanent home in New York City. The exhibit opened at Luna Park, a brand-new amusement park on Coney Island.
Couney and Nurse Maye married that September. Their exhibit quickly became one of Coney Island's most popular attractions.
WITH
LIVING INFA
Babies! Don't forget to see the babies! Only 25 cents!
In a single weekend, people visited by the tens of thousands!
WITH
LIVING INFANTS

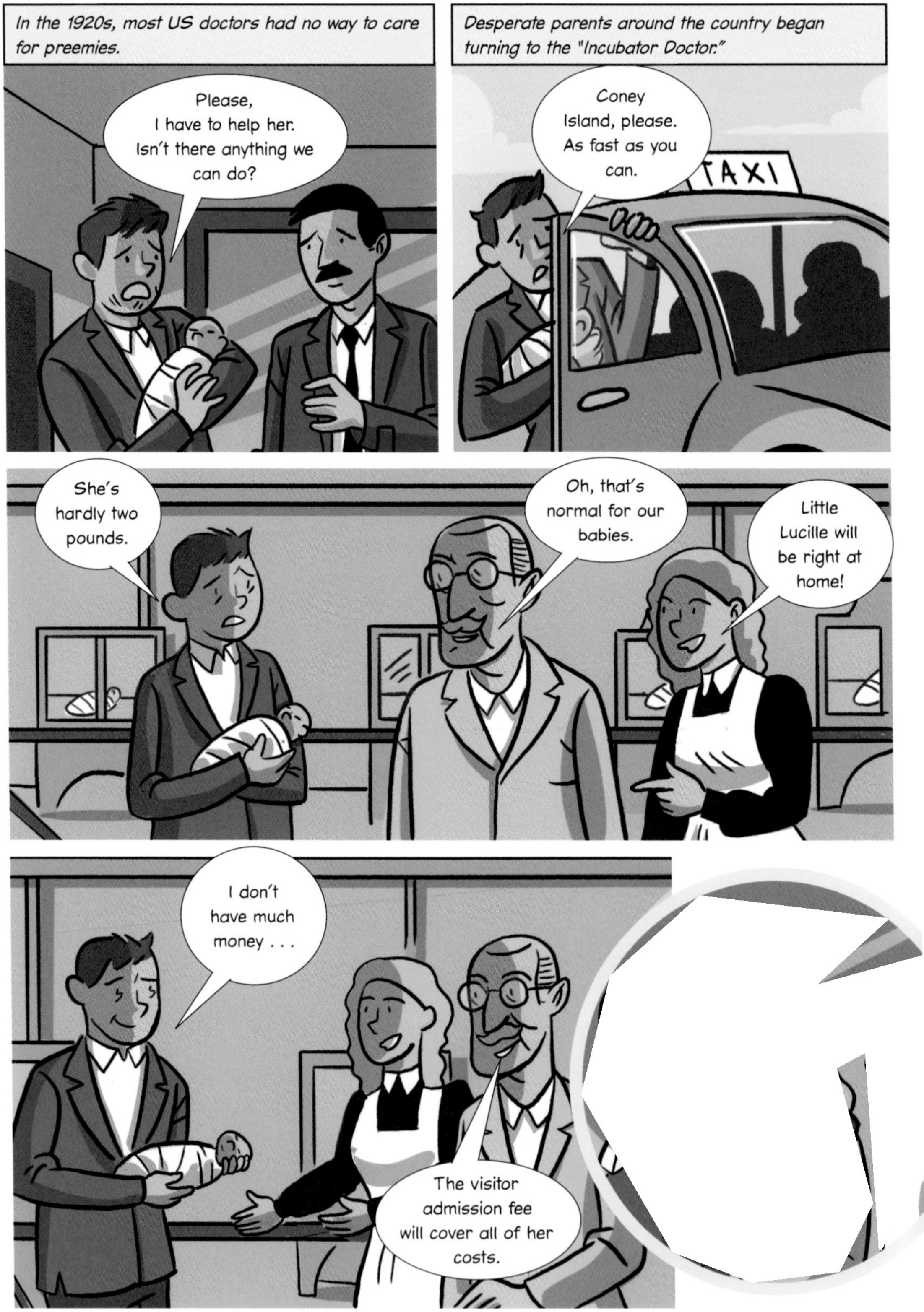
In the 1920s, most US doctors had no way to care for preemies.
Please, I have to help her. Isn't there anything we can do?
Desperate parents around the country began turning to the "Incubator Doctor."
Coney Island, please. As fast as you can.
TAXI
She's hardly two pounds.
Oh, that's normal for our babies.
Little Lucille will be right at home!
I don't have much money . . .
The visitor admission fee will cover all of her costs.

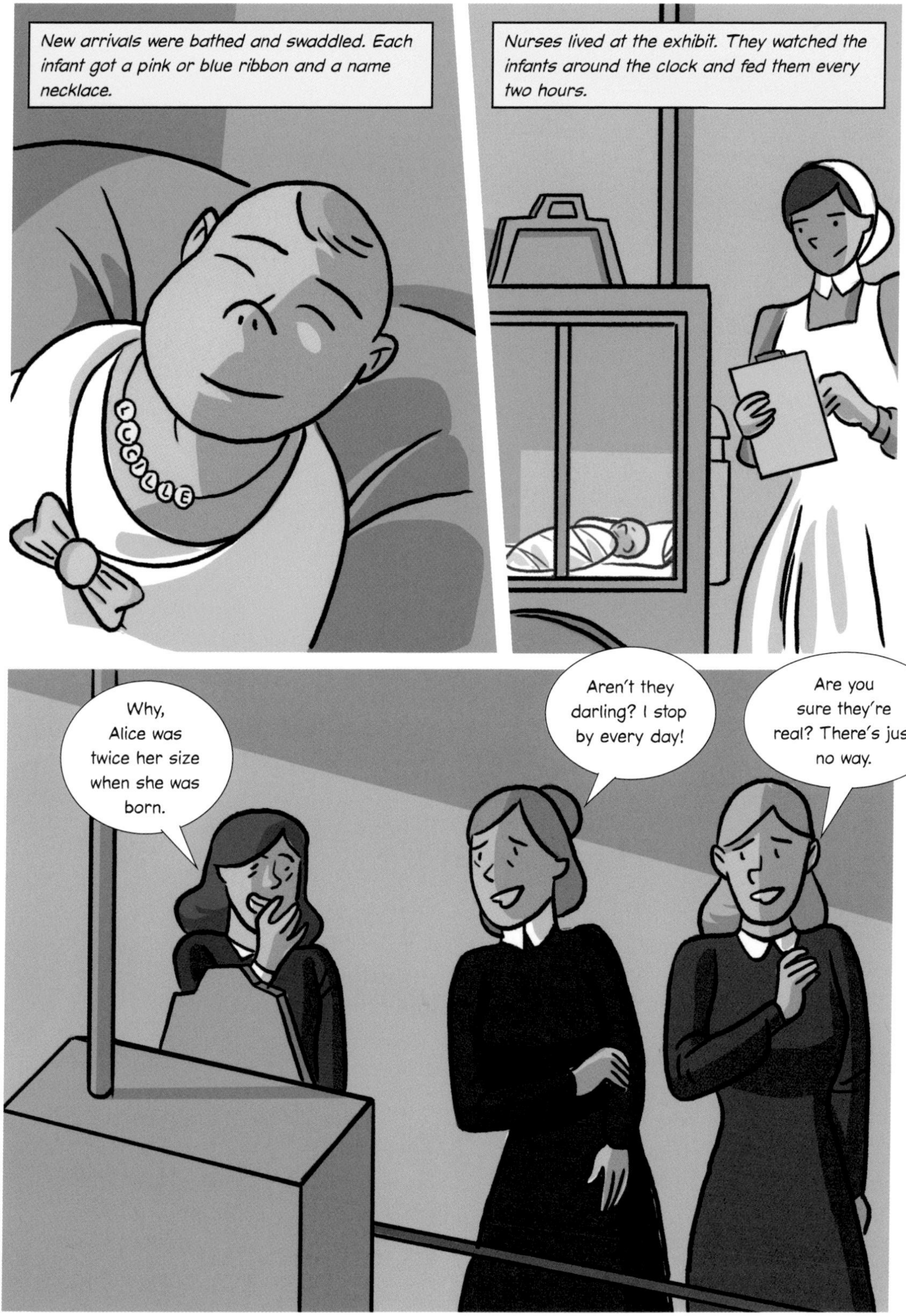
New arrivals were bathed and swaddled. Each infant got a pink or blue ribbon and a name necklace.
LUCILLE
Nurses lived at the exhibit. They watched the infants around the clock and fed them every two hours.
Why, Alice was twice her size when she was born.
Aren't they darling? I stop by every day!
Are you sure they're real? There's just no way.

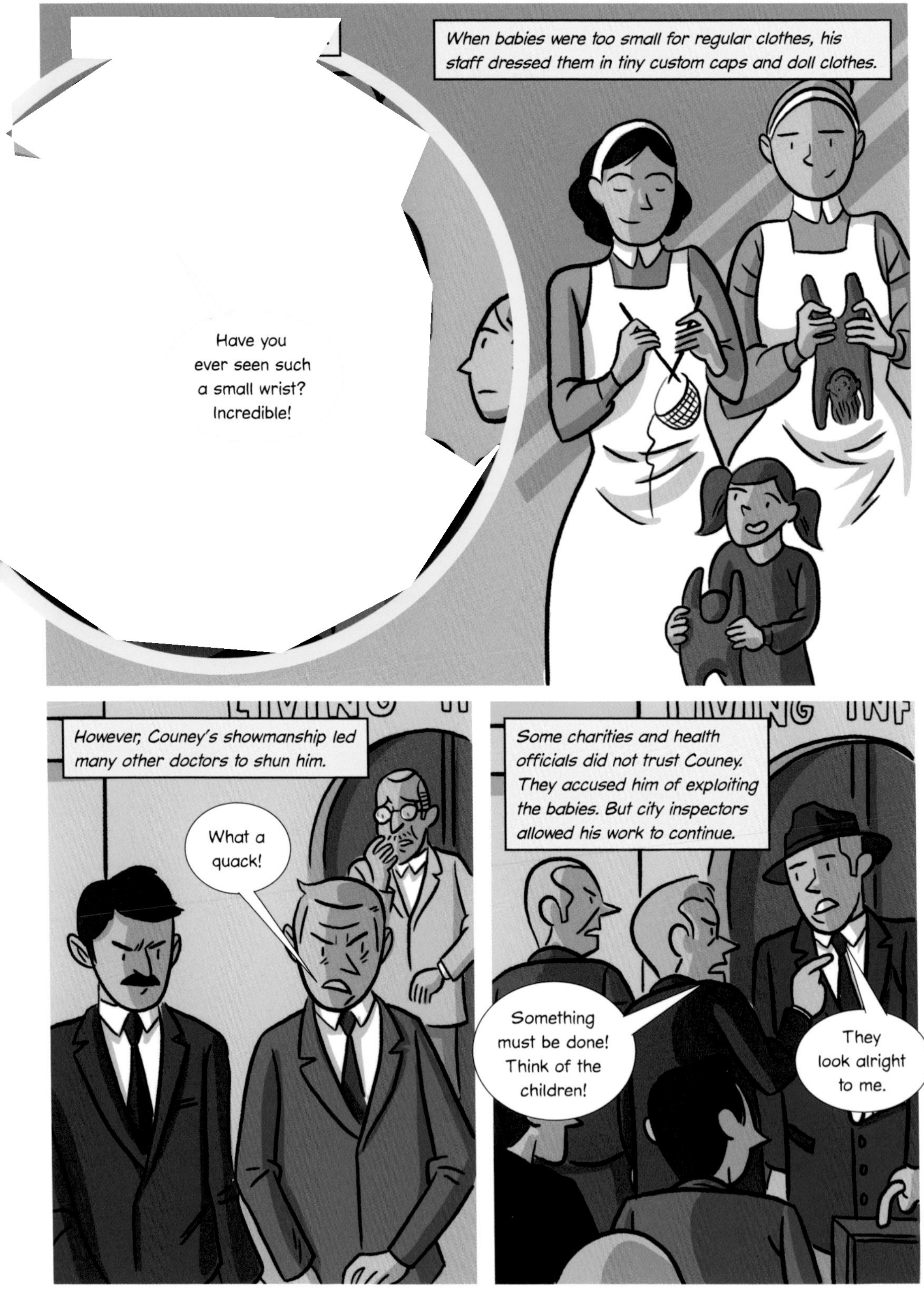
Have you ever seen such a small wrist? Incredible!
When babies were too small for regular clothes, his staff dressed them in tiny custom caps and doll clothes.
However, Couney's showmanship led many other doctors to shun him.
What a quack!
Some charities and health officials did not trust Couney. They accused him of exploiting the babies. But city inspectors allowed his work to continue.
Something must be done! Think of the children!
They look alright to me.

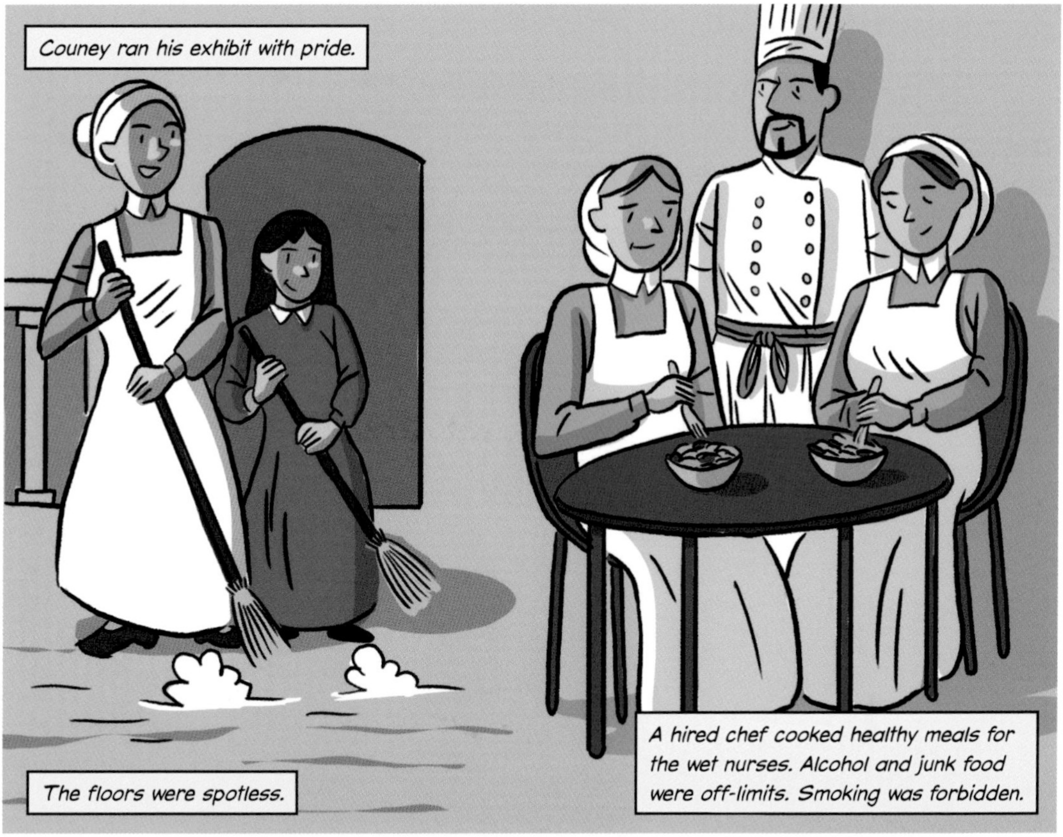
Couney ran his exhibit with pride.
The floors were spotless.
A hired chef cooked healthy meals for the wet nurses. Alcohol and junk food were off-limits. Smoking was forbidden.

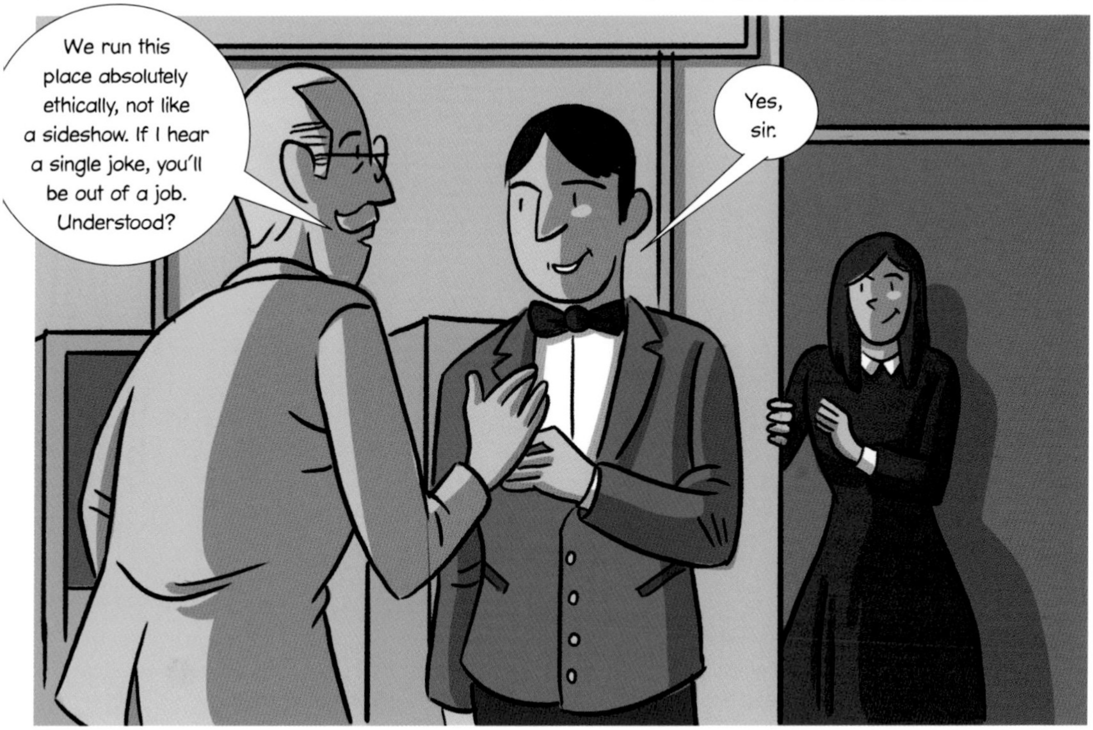
We run this place absolutely ethically, not like a sideshow. If I hear a single joke, you'll be out of a job. Understood?
Yes, sir.

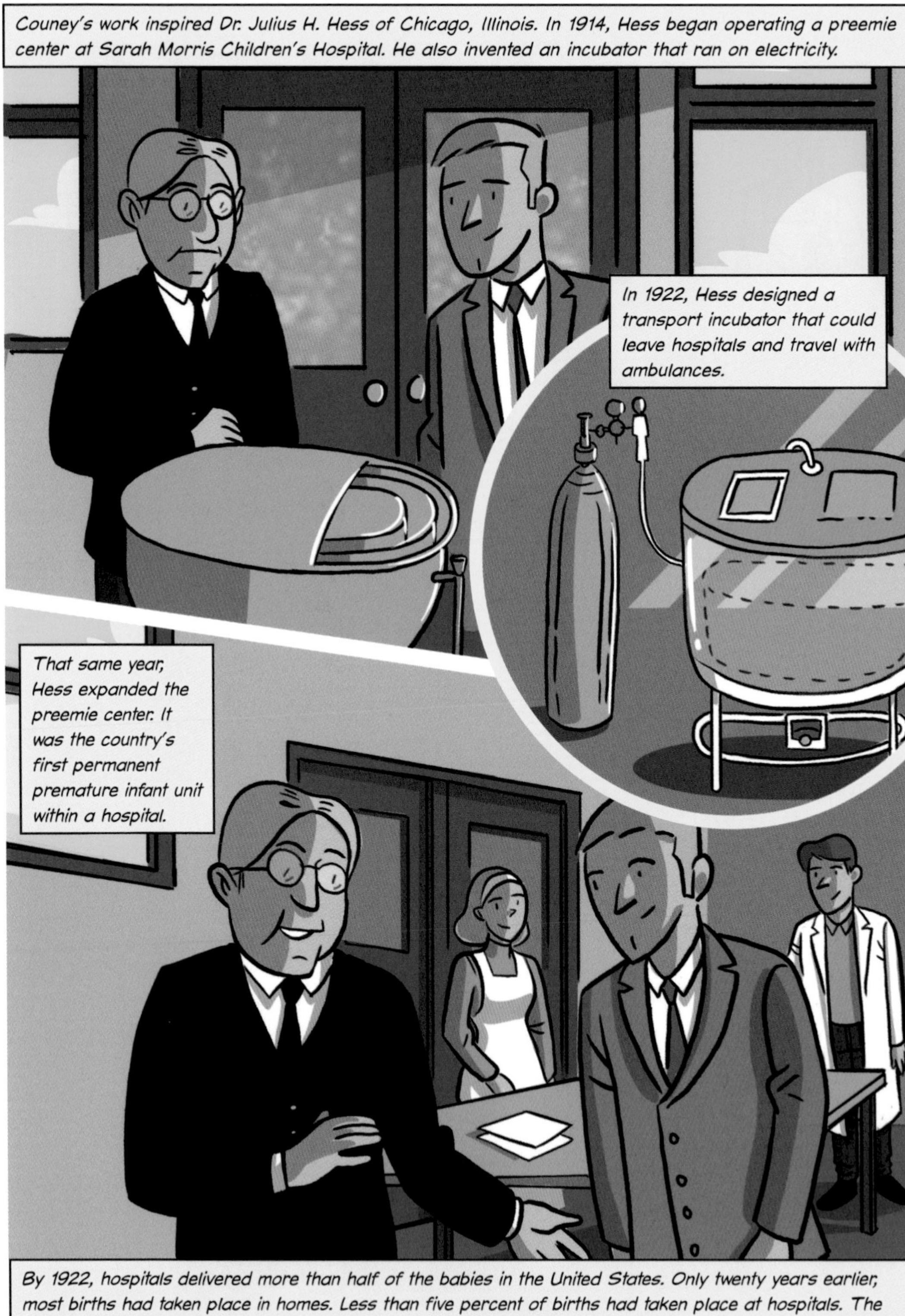
Couney's work inspired Dr. Julius H. Hess of Chicago, Illinois. In 1914, Hess began operating a preemie center at Sarah Morris Children's Hospital. He also invented an incubator that ran on electricity.
In 1922, Hess designed a transport incubator that could leave hospitals and travel with ambulances.
That same year, Hess expanded the preemie center. It was the country's first permanent premature infant unit within a hospital.
By 1922, hospitals delivered more than half of the babies in the United States. Only twenty years earlier, most births had taken place in homes. Less than five percent of births had taken place at hospitals. The preemie center was building a reputation for science and safety. Families were taking notice.

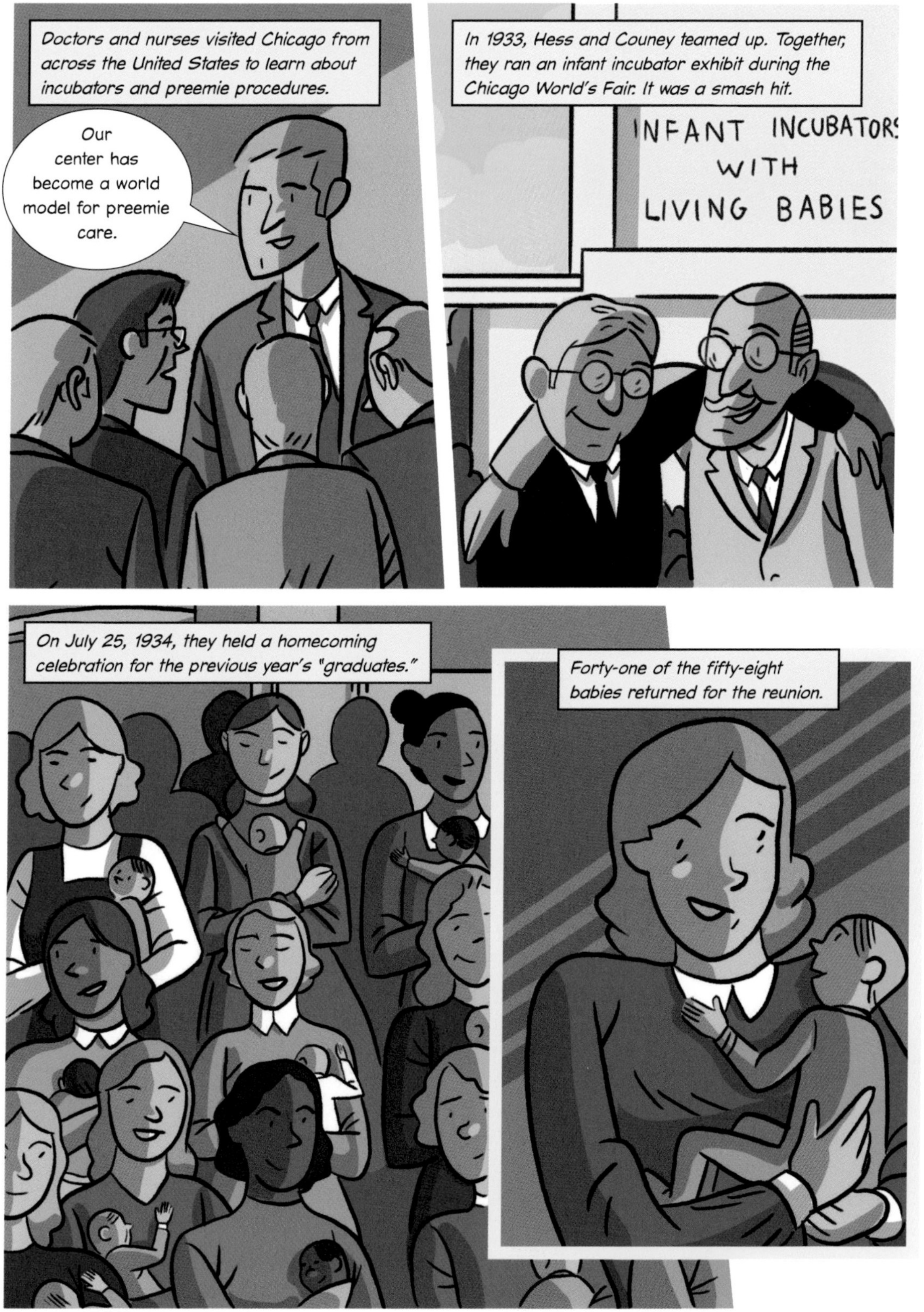
Doctors and nurses visited Chicago from across the United States to learn about incubators and preemie procedures.
Our center has become a world model for preemie care.
In 1933, Hess and Couney teamed up. Together, they ran an infant incubator exhibit during the Chicago World's Fair. It was a smash hit.
INFANT INCUBATORS WITH LIVING BABIES
On July 25, 1934, they held a homecoming celebration for the previous year's "graduates."
Forty-one of the fifty-eight babies returned for the reunion.

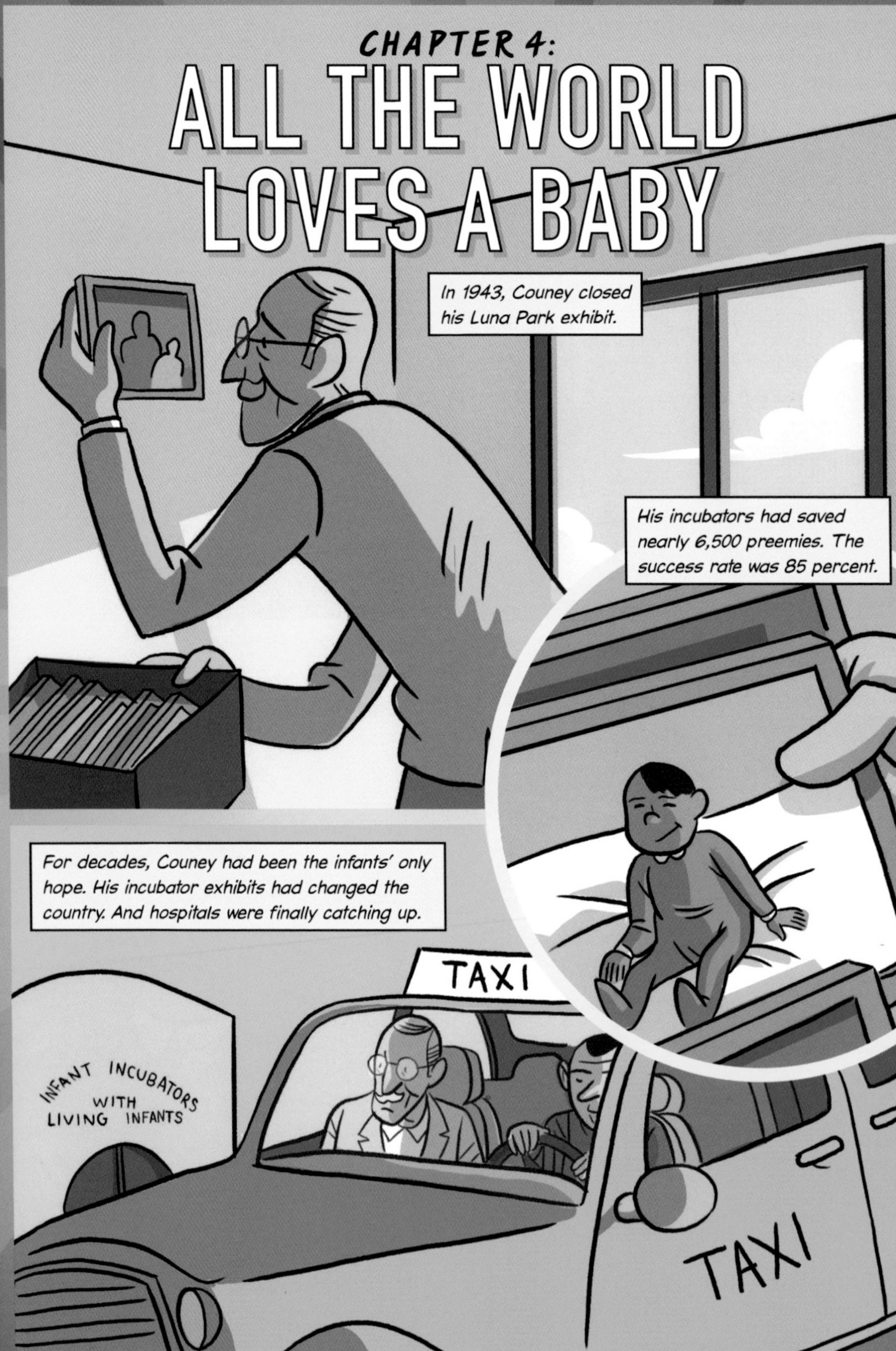
CHAPTER 4:
ALL THE WORLD LOVES A BABY
In 1943, Couney closed his Luna Park exhibit.
His incubators had saved nearly 6,500 preemies. The success rate was 85 percent.
For decades, Couney had been the infants' only hope. His incubator exhibits had changed the country. And hospitals were finally catching up.
TAXI
INFANT INCUBATORS WITH LIVING INFANTS
TAXI

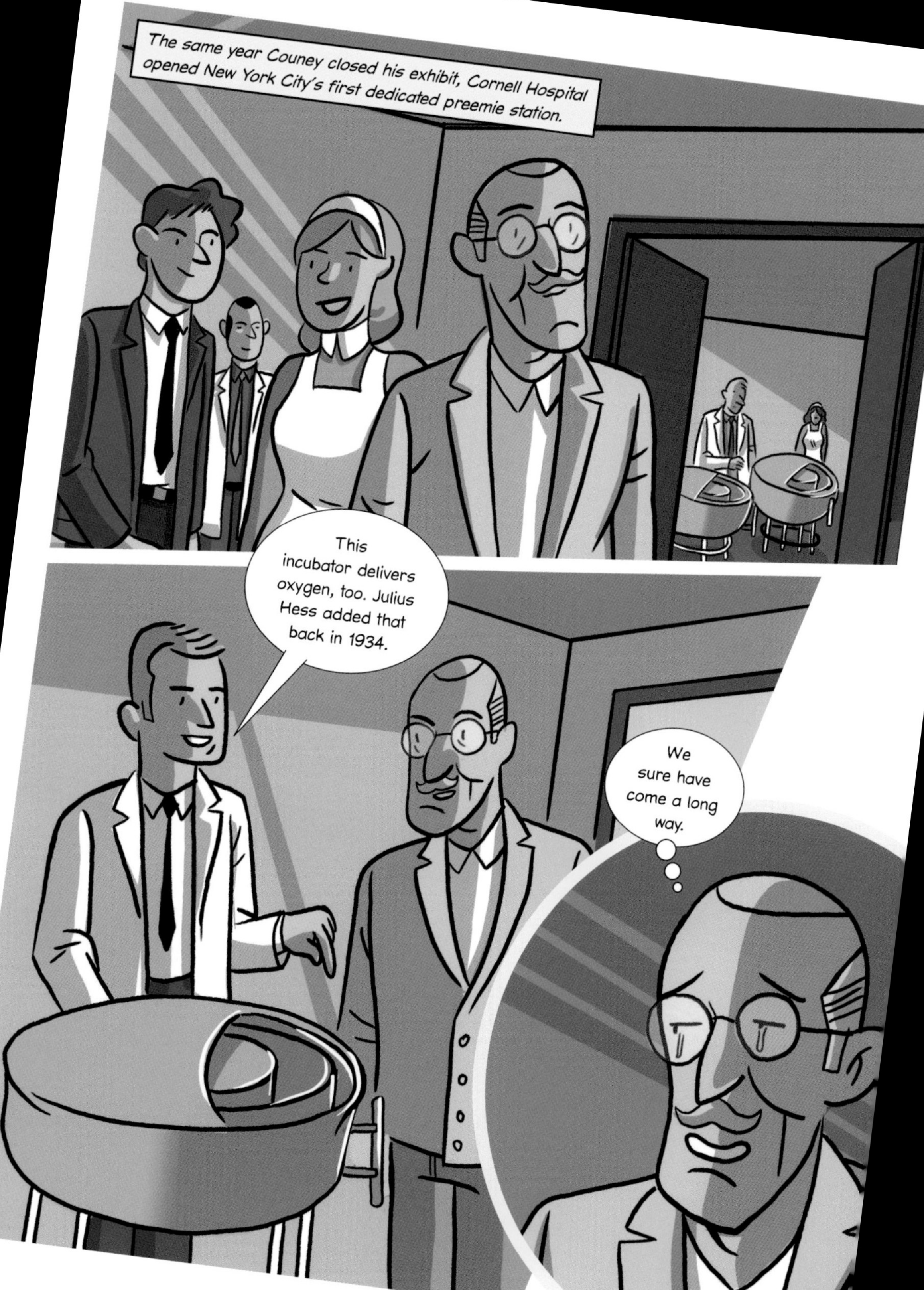
The same year Couney closed his exhibit, Cornell Hospital opened New York City's first dedicated preemie station.
This incubator delivers oxygen, too. Julius Hess added that back in 1934.
We sure have come a long way.

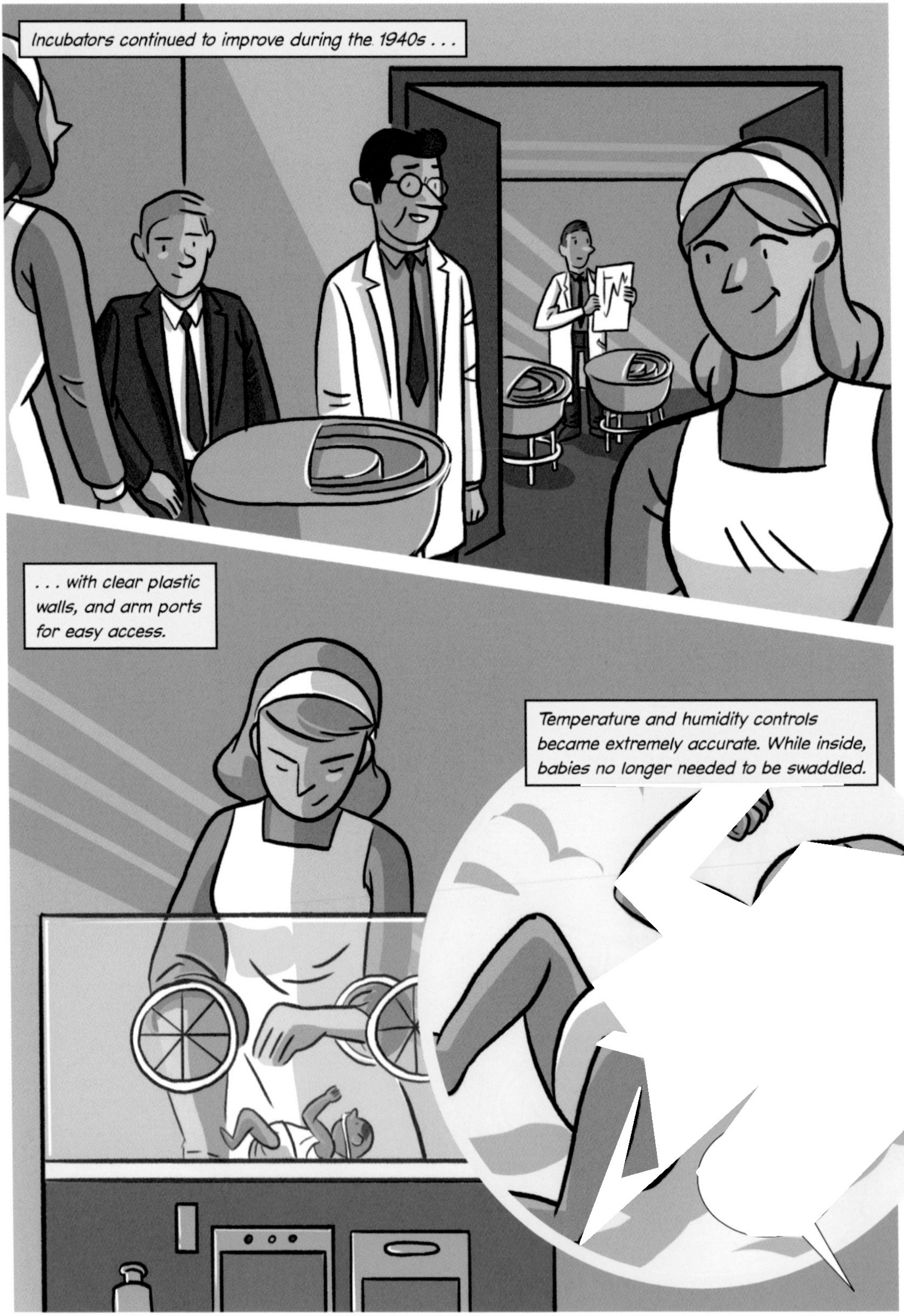
Incubators continued to improve during the 1940s . . .
. . . with clear plastic walls, and arm ports for easy access.
Temperature and humidity controls became extremely accurate. While inside, babies no longer needed to be swaddled.

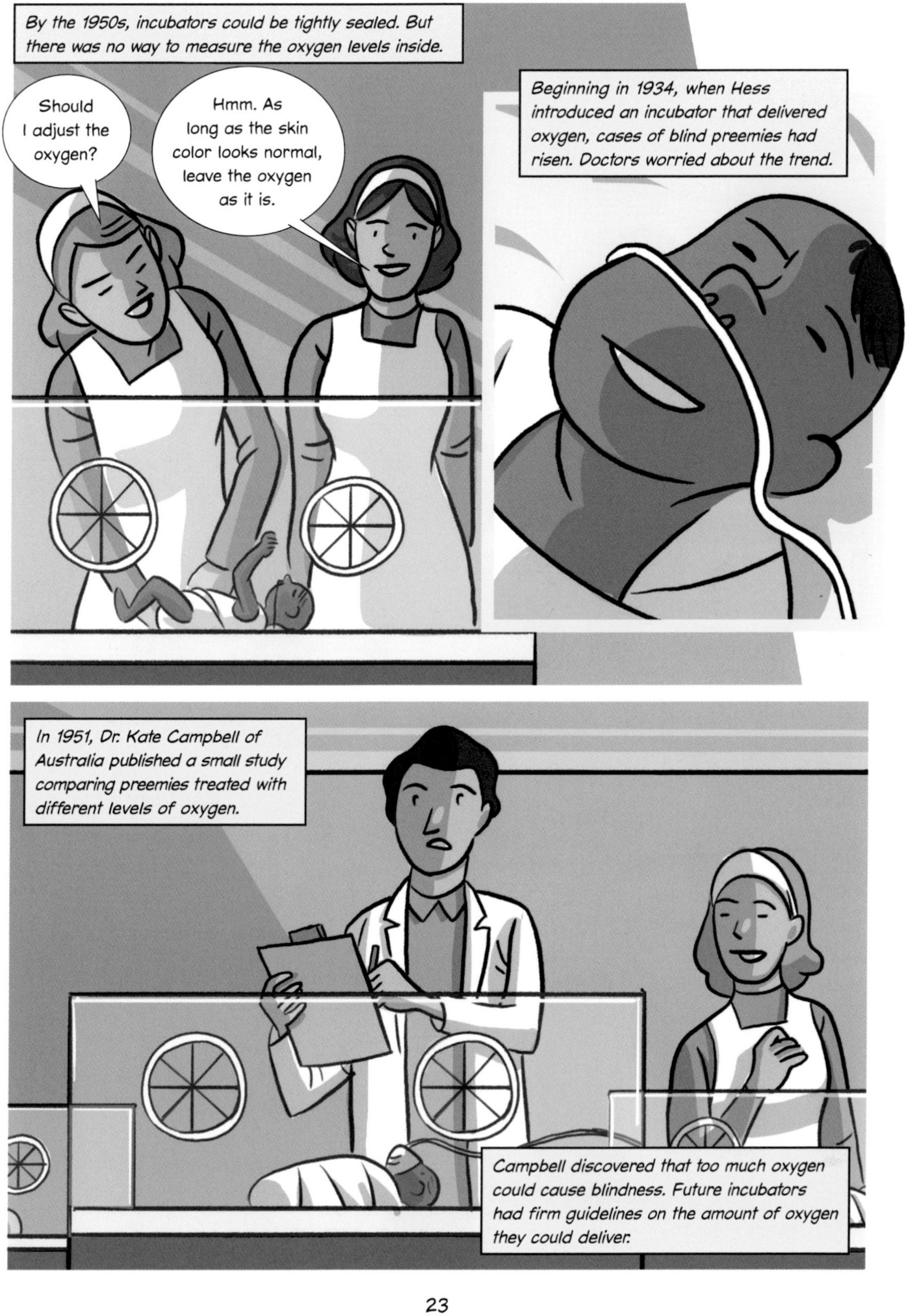
By the 1950s, incubators could be tightly sealed. But there was no way to measure the oxygen levels inside.
Should I adjust the oxygen?
Hmm. As long as the skin color looks normal, leave the oxygen as it is.
Beginning in 1934, when Hess introduced an incubator that delivered oxygen, cases of blind preemies had risen. Doctors worried about the trend.
In 1951, Dr. Kate Campbell of Australia published a small study comparing preemies treated with different levels of oxygen.
Campbell discovered that too much oxygen could cause blindness. Future incubators had firm guidelines on the amount of oxygen they could deliver.

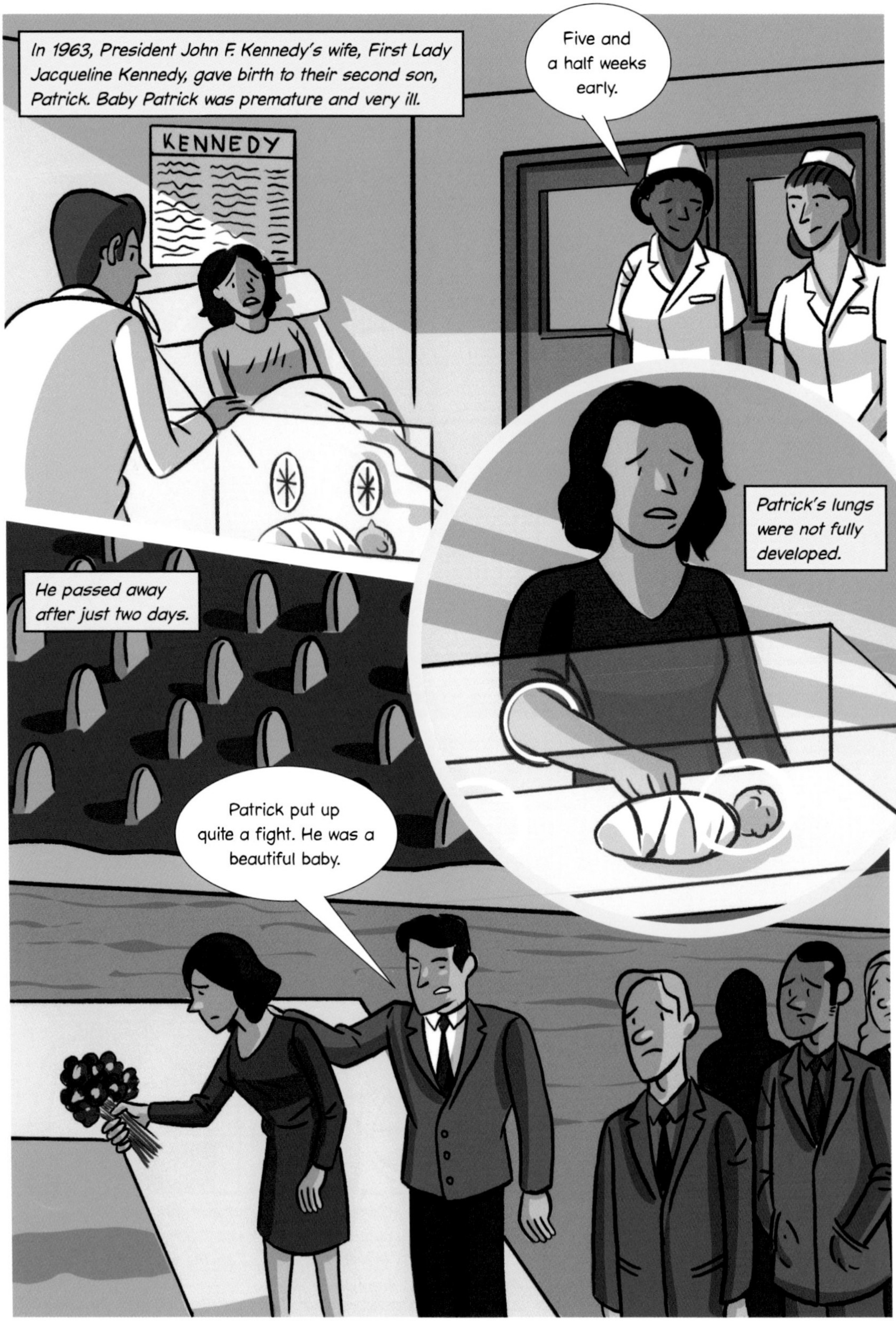
In 1963, President John F. Kennedy's wife, First Lady Jacqueline Kennedy, gave birth to their second son, Patrick. Baby Patrick was premature and very ill.
KENNEDY
Five and a half weeks early.
Patrick's lungs were not fully developed.
He passed away after just two days.
Patrick put up quite a fight. He was a beautiful baby.

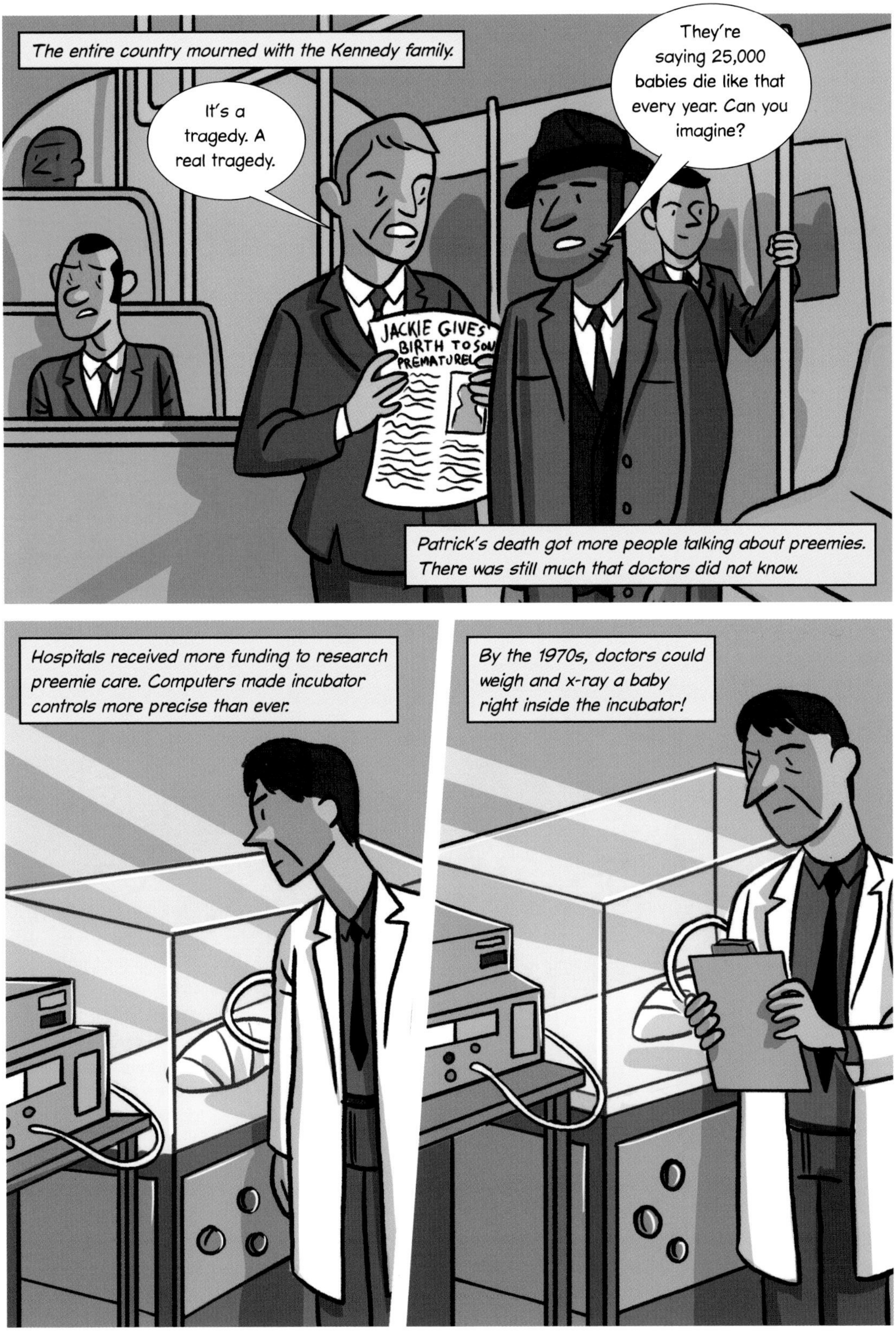
The entire country mourned with the Kennedy family.
It's a tragedy. A real tragedy.
They're saying 25,000 babies die like that every year. Can you imagine?
JACKIE GIVES BIRTH TO SON PREMATUREL
Patrick's death got more people talking about preemies. There was still much that doctors did not know.
Hospitals received more funding to research preemie care. Computers made incubator controls more precise than ever.
By the 1970s, doctors could weigh and x-ray a baby right inside the incubator!

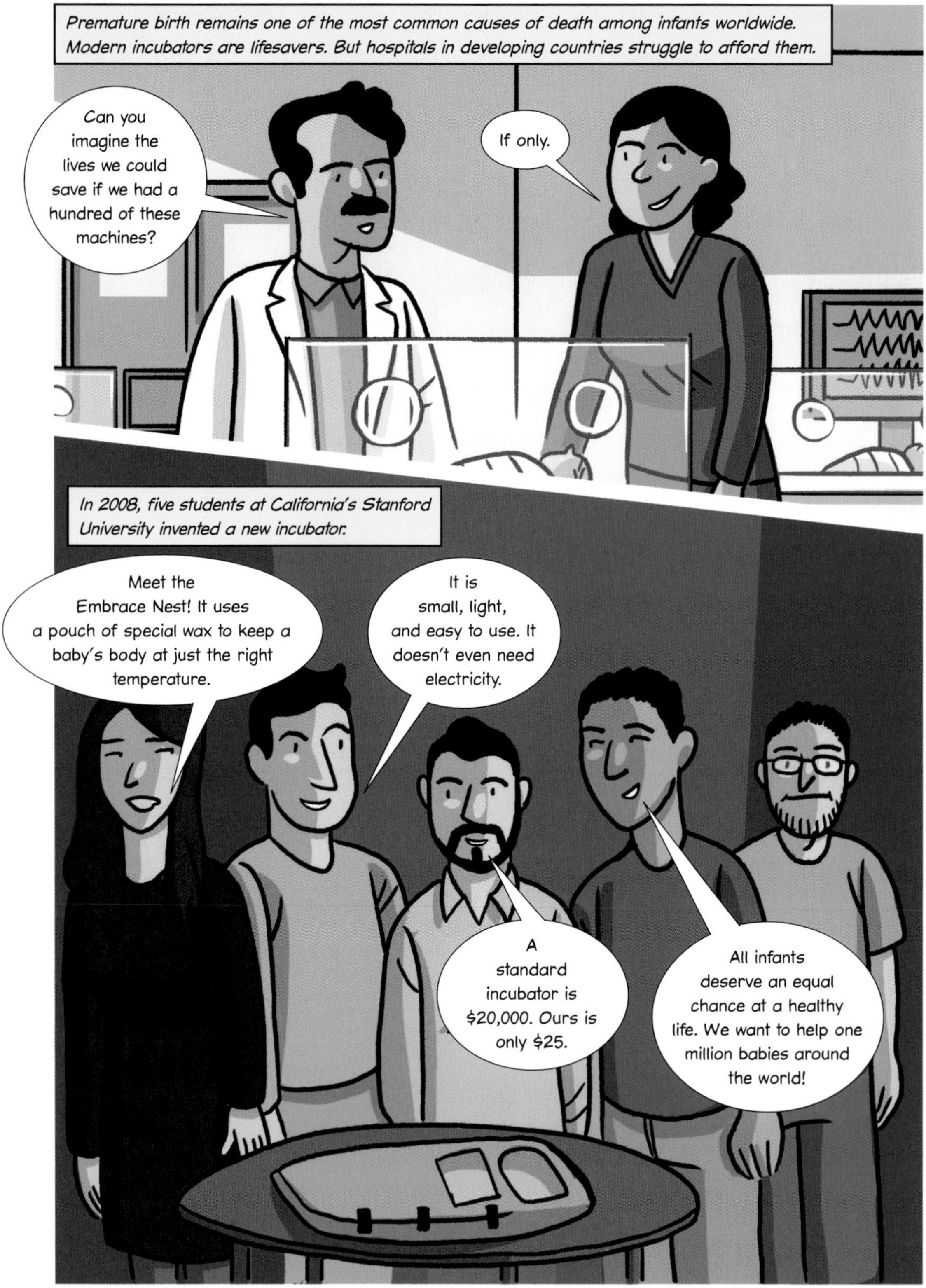
Premature birth remains one of the most common causes of death among infants worldwide. Modern incubators are lifesavers. But hospitals in developing countries struggle to afford them.
Can you imagine the lives we could save if we had a hundred of these machines?
If only.
In 2008, five students at California's Stanford University invented a new incubator.
Meet the Embrace Nest! It uses a pouch of special wax to keep a baby's body at just the right temperature.
It is small, light, and easy to use. It doesn't even need electricity.
A standard incubator is $20,000. Ours is only $25.
All infants deserve an equal chance at a healthy life. We want to help one million babies around the world!

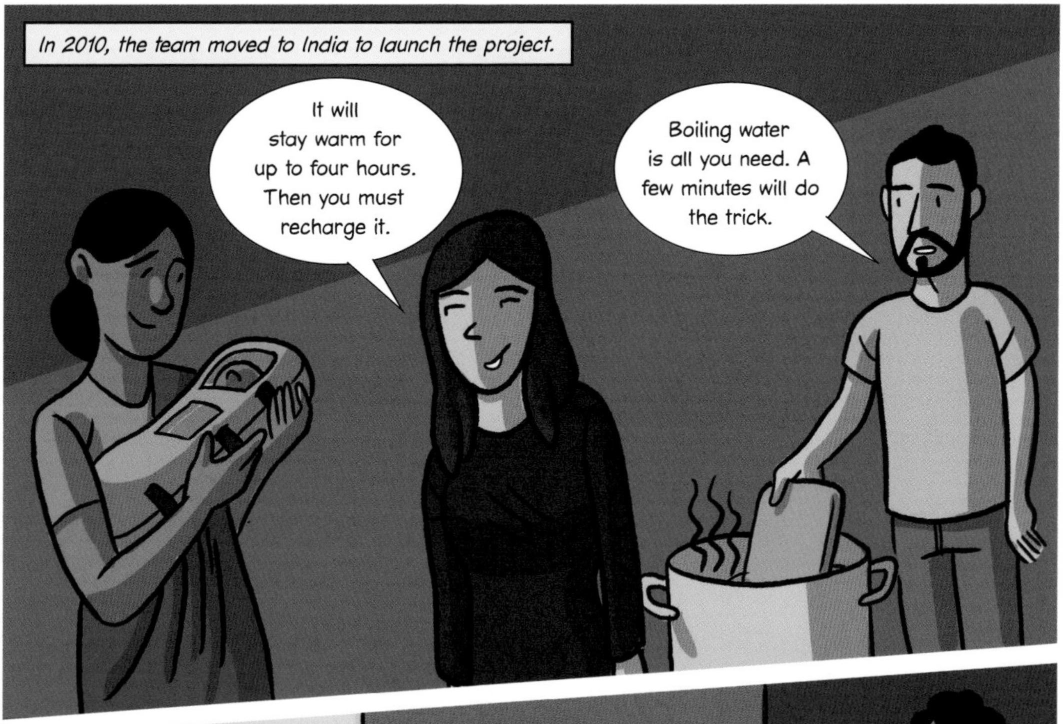
In 2010, the team moved to India to launch the project.
It will stay warm for up to four hours. Then you must recharge it.
Boiling water is all you need. A few minutes will do the trick.

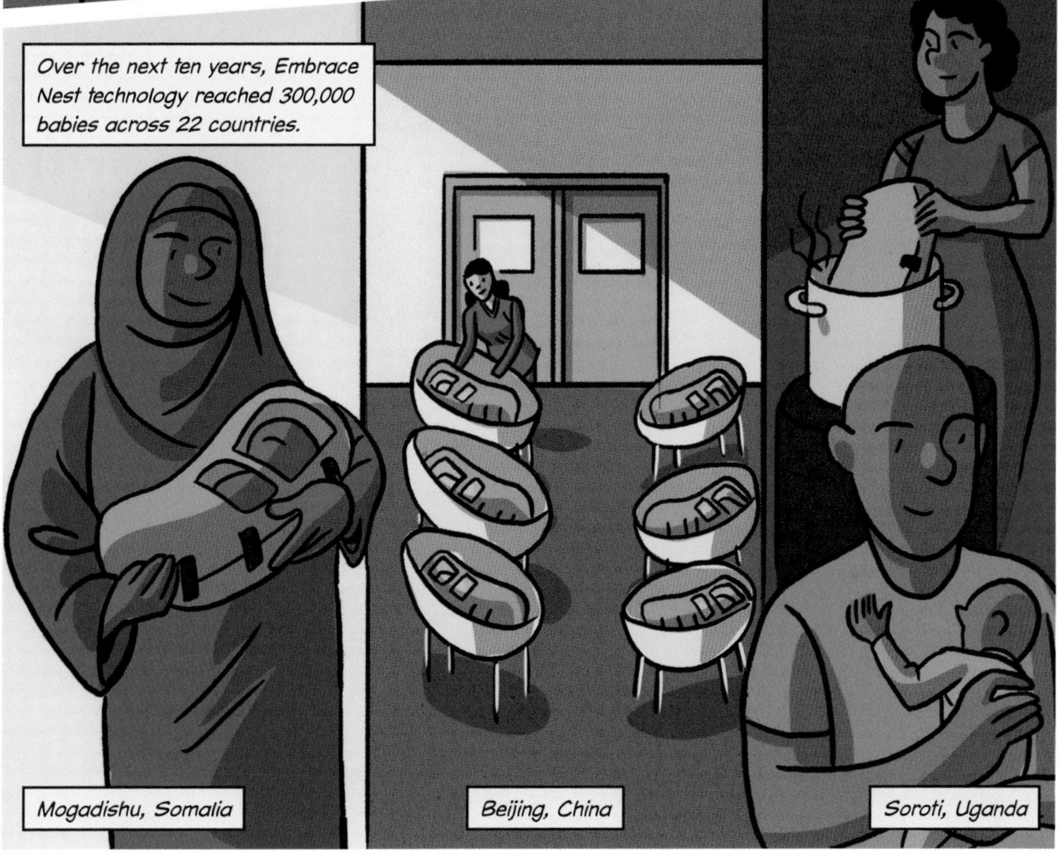
Over the next ten years, Embrace Nest technology reached 300,000 babies across 22 countries.
Mogadishu, Somalia
Beijing, China
Soroti, Uganda

Fifteen million preemies enter the world every year. That is about twenty-eight babies each minute!

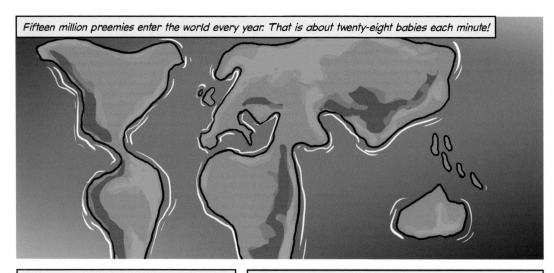

Some are born as early as fourteen weeks premature. Incubators give them a fighting chance at life.

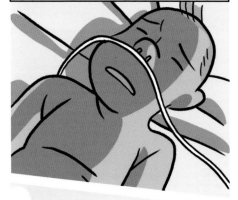

Incubators have come a long way from hatching chickens and drawing crowds.

But they continue to do what they have always done: change the lives of families forever!

SOURCE NOTES

11   Dawn Raffel, *The Strange Case of Dr. Couney: How a Mysterious European Showman Saved Thousands of American Babies* (New York: Blue Rider Press, 2018).

GLOSSARY

allergen: a substance that causes an allergic reaction, such as pollen

developing country: a poorer country with a weak or less developed economy

device: a piece of equipment with a special purpose

exhibit: a public show

Franco-German War: a war between the French and Prussian Empires that occurred from 1870 to 1871

graduate: a person who successfully graduates from school with a degree or diploma

hatchery: a place for hatching eggs

humidity: the measure of how much water is in the air

infection: a disease caused by bacteria that enter the body

maternity: providing care before and after childbirth

oxygen: a gas that makes up 21 percent of the air

patient: a person who receives medical treatment

population: the total number of people living in a country or region

premature: arriving before the proper time

quack: somebody who practices medicine dishonestly

surgery: a medical procedure that requires operating on a patient

swaddle: to wrap a baby tightly in clothes or blankets

temperature: the measure of hot or cold

thermostat: a device for measuring how hot or cold a space is

wet nurse: a woman who cares for and breastfeeds babies

womb: the organ in which babies grow

x-ray: to photograph an object using x-ray technology

FURTHER INFORMATION

Britannica Kids—Incubator
https://kids.britannica.com/students/article/incubator/275041

Farndon, John. *Stickmen's Guide to Technology*. Minneapolis: Hungry Tomato, 2018.

Fiske, Anna. *How Do You Make a Baby?* Wellington, NZ: Gecko Press, 2020.

KidsHealth—Welcoming a New Baby into Your Family
https://kidshealth.org/en/kids/new-baby.html?ref=search

The Kinderhearted Classroom—Hatching Chicks in the Classroom
https://www.youtube.com/watch?v=pyBNZfZmyqU

Neonatology on the Web—Coney Island Sideshows
http://www.neonatology.org/pinups/coneyislandnurses.html

INDEX